FRENCH
AND
NATIVE
NORTH AMERICAN
MARRIAGES
1600-1800

Paul J. Bunnell, FACG, UE

HERITAGE BOOKS
2004

HERITAGE BOOKS

AN IMPRINT OF HERITAGE BOOKS, INC.

Books, CDs, and more – Worldwide

For our listing of thousands of titles see our website
at
www.HeritageBooks.com

Ancient Huron beadwork shown on the cover of this book is from
Four Huron Wampam Records, by E. B. Taylor, 1897
Feathers Copyright © 2005 by artist Matthew Paul Bunnell

Published 2004 by
HERITAGE BOOKS, INC.
Publishing Division
65 East Main Street
Westminster, Maryland 21157-5026

International Standard Book Number: **0-7884-2595-1**

Loyalty is Everything

**This work is dedicated to my Huron ancestors
to whom I am related, in some cases, several times**

Nicolas Arendanki/Anenontha (Huron) of the "Bear Clan."
Married:
Jeanne Otrihouandt/Otrihandit/Otrihoandit (Huron) "Bear
Clan," whose daughter was:
Catherine Annenontha/Annenontak who married #1 Jean Durand
and #2 Jacques Couturier who had Genevieve Couturier.

****

Joachim Arontio Ouentouen (Huron) possibly "Bear Clan."
Married:
Cecile/Celine Arenhatsi/Arendaeronnon (Huron) "People of the
Rock," whose daughter was:
Marie-Felix Ouentouen/Arontio, who married Laurant
Dubeau/Duboc

****

Germain Doucet (Possibly Micmac, more research needed)
Married:
Marie Jeanne Bourgeois whose son was Pierre Doucet who
married Henriette Pelletret, possible Metis through her mother. And
through their daughter, Marguaret Louise-Judith Ducet who married
Abraham Dugas.

****

Jean Claude Landry (Micmac)
Married:
Marie Sale/Salle
Whose daughter was Antoinette who married Antoine Bourg.

****

Marie Daussey/Doucet (Native, needs more research)
Married:
Jean/Jehan Guadet
Whose daughter was Marie Anne Gaudet who married Etienne
Hebert.

****

Martin Aucoin
Married:
A Metis Woman (Needs more research, one record of daughter,
Michelle says he was a Metis? She married Michel Boudrot). And
through daughter, Jeannine Aucoin who married ??

****

Pierre Lejeune
Married:
A MicMac/Mi'qnak Woman
Whose daughter was Edmee Lejeune who married Francois
Gaudreau.

****

Radegode (MicMac oral history says she was of First Nation
People)
Married:
Jehan/Jean Lambert
Whose daughter, Jeanne Radegonde Lambert who married
Jean/Jehan Blanchard.

****

Recognition

The following recognition is worth the mention from this author because of their hard work and dedication to the discovery, identification and corrections to our First Nation and Metis families. I thank them all.

Metis in Québec and Eastern Canada
http://www.metisduquebec.ca/

Norm Léveillée of West Greenwich, Rhode Island
http://www.leveillee.net/ancestry/ and
http://www.leveillee.net/roots/

"Programme de recherché en demographie historique" from the University of Montreal, Quebec (PRDH)

Dictionaire Genealogique Des Familles Acadiennes, English Supplement by Stephen White, published 2000 by Centre D'Etudes Acadiennes, Part I, 1636 to 1711. (And his added correction materials.)

Gail Morin Metis Families, of Elmer, Washington
http://www.televar.com/~gmorin/vandal.htm

American-Canadian Genealogical Society, Manchester, NH
www.acgs.org

Other Heritage Books by Paul J. Bunnell:

The New Loyalist Index, Volume I

The New Loyalist Index Volume II

The New Loyalist Index, Volume III, Including Cape Cod & Islands, Massachusetts, New Hampshire, New Jersey and New York Loyalists

The House of Robinson. The Robinsons of Rhode Island: Their Genealogy & Letters, and The History of the Robinson & Son Oil Company of Baltimore, Maryland

Thunder Over New England: Benjamin Bonnell, The Loyalist. A Loyalist Story & Family Genealogy Including Other Loyalist Bunnell/Bonnell Genealogies

Research Guide To Loyalist Ancestors: A Directory To Archives, Manuscripts, Published and Electronic Sources (Updated and Revised)

Cemetery Inscriptions of the Town of Barnstable, Massachusetts, and its Villages, 1600-1900, with Corrections and Additions

Loyalist Migrations & Documents Guide

Acadian & Cajun Cooking & Old Remedies The Way Memere Made Them

Life of a Haunted House. The Barnstable House of Barnstable, Massachusetts: Genealogy of A Real Haunted House

Preface

I compiled this book because of the need to identify the mixed marriages in Canada between mostly the French and Canadian North American Indian population during the early settlement years. (In some cases there are some non-French records). This material can help others establish their proud Indian heritage. Unfortunately, the Native North American people did not record their genealogy, but only in oral tradition, so nearly all marriages, births, baptisms and deaths will at best have their parents listed from French records. There is very little knowledge beyond that first generation.

I have also added single people listings as in baptisms or census records from convents, etc. This could possibly show a person before they married a Non-Native North American or attempt to establish a family member. The people with no last names were listed at the beginning of this book or under Sauvages (ees) (Savage). I have also tried to list the French surname first where one was available, as in a marriage record. Following that surname will be the Native North American's names as it was recorded, ending with their given first name by the French, usually a Christian name. Where other names or tribes are recorded I will list them too.

Every attempt has been made to capture all records in the various sources listed here. I apologize if any have been missed. Any corrections or additions reported, with the proper sources will be posted on my website. Where I could not translate, I entered the French language. Some marriage locations are not given. 99% of the cases recorded are from Quebec or Acadie (New Brunswick, Maine, Nova Scotia, PEI). The surname "Sauvage" and "Sauvageau" are questionable as being Indian because many are not.

I left this name out in nearly all cases because so many had the name without proof of Indian descent hoping it was not a major error. But, the surnames of Sauvages or Sauvageese are Indian labels.

Where there is no last name, these people are listed under the above descriptions. Many of these listings have no marriages but could connect to some French families by matching the vital statistics, possibly later on.

There were many listings of people being (Origin, from Acadie) "d'origine Acadienne." not necessarily of Indian descent. All the surnames with the number 8 in them are Native names. The French used an 8 because of pronunciation problems in the French language. The sound is: "ooh."

There are some cases where I listed a Native North American married to another Indian. This was done to record that marriage in case of intermarriage later. I also listed birth and or baptism record of a single people because they may have a married to French lines later. In these cases, birth, baptism, locations or surname could help match. Some records are noted in French where I could not translate.

Some births may be baptisms because of errors made in translation from French to English. Where I noted nee and ne is probably the births, and the "b" is baptisms. Please excuse my lack of a proper French education. It is something I wish my mother had taught me as a child while I attended French Catholic School during my first year at Secret Heart Catholic Church in Amesbury, Massachusetts.

It is very important to note that many of the early sources had errors, some in translation. The works of Jette, Tanguay and Arseneault are just a few to watch out for. There are corrections out there as in the cae of Steven White's Dictionnaire. The corrections in this printing would not have been created without the hard work and dedication of Norm Léveillée. It is always good to cross check when possible. Any futher corrections will be posted on my website:

http://www.bunnellgenealogybooks.citymaker.com

Good luck and I hope that you find your Native North American Ancestors.

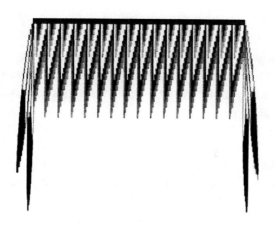

LAKOTA FOREVER

*If I could talk to my Great-Grandfathers,
I would say the old times are gone.
So much has changed,
But love, like the wind, is still here.*

*When all else fades away,
Faith, Hope and Love will remain.*

*Those feelings that are so strong and so
strange,
Will always be with us.*

*I think of you my relatives,
And, I thank you; I thank you.*

Composed by Paul Leroche, of Brule (pka Brule), CD
1996, "We The People."

Source Codes

The following source codes are listed after each entry on the last line as, "Source." In many cases there may be several sources noted. If any errors or misstatements are found, please contact the author.

AMD –
Acadian Metis Descendants (Genweb Index) on website http://freepages.genealogy.rootsweb.com/~metisgen/db11/ dated 17 Dec. 2002

BG -
"Bernard Genealogy," by Henry T. Peterson Jr., 2003, published on website

BKR –
Betty Kienitz (a.k.a. Menogeshickquay, "Good Sky Woman") genealogy records

CAF –
Canadian Archive Files. Reference RG15, Interior, Series D-11-8-a, Volume 1319, Reel C-14926, File Title: "Scrip affidavit for Josette Carriere, wife of Moise Carriere"

CENSUS 1671 -
Port Royal, Acadie (Nova Scotia)

CENSUS 1686 -
Port Royal, Acadie (Nova Scotia)

DGA -
Website http://www.telusplanet.net/public/dgarnea/direct.htm or http://www.agt.net/public/dgarneau dated March 2003

DGDFA Eng Sup –
Dictionaire Genealogique Des Familles Acadiennes, English Supplement by Stephen White, published 2000 by Centre D'Etudes Acadiennes, Part I, 1636 to 1711

DNCF –
Dictionaire National des Canadiens Francais 1608-1760, by Institute of Drouin, 2 volumes, published by Siege Social, Montreal, Canada 1985

DGDFA –
Dictionaire Genealogique Des Familles Acadiennes (The Genealogy Dictionary of Acadian Families) by Stephen A. White, published by Centre D'Etudes Acadiennes, 1999. 2 vols., in French

DRU –
Druoin Book, 1977, page 1108

FQM -
Montagnais genealogy found: http://www.francogene.com/quebec/montagnais.html provided by Serge Goudreau, page about Quebec's Amerindians and Metis dated 24 Jan. 2003

GFH -
From website grandesfamilies.org/Hyard/02.html dated March 2003

GMMF –
Gail Morin Metis Families, of Elmer, Washington. http://www.televar.com/~gmorin/vandal.htm This site has a lot of hard work put into it by Gail and it covers much materials on the Metis Families. (22 Feb. 2003). Gail references all sources she consulted on each surname.

HH –
"Huron History" (article), by Lee Sultzman, 10 Feb. 2000

JBDF –
"Chief Joseph Brant UE," article published 1995 by Donald J. Flowers, UE, Toronto, Canada

JR –
From the Jette marriage records

JRAD –
Jesuit Relations and Allied Documents. Vol. 1, 1610-1791. (Some records were recorded here only if there was an age or chance of a future marriage to a French settler.)

LEV–
Léveillée Ancestry genealogy site on Internet, produced by Norm Léveillée of West Greenwich, Rhode Island. His assistance help verify or correct several areas in this revised edition. This source ID (LEV) has been added to listings that were corrected or verified. Norm's Internet site is: http://www.leveillee.net/ancestry/ and http://www.leveillee.net/roots/. He has dedicated the early collection of family records to Rita Jeanne Léveillée, his sister, plus invaluable material and guidance from his cousin, Suzanne Boivin Sommerville. You can find some of her work at site: http://www.leveillee.net/roots/index.html. He cited another excellent secondary site, http://www.genealogy.umontreal.ca that identifies errors made in the Tanguay and Jette books, along with another contributor, Jean Quintal who sent him primary sources on his Algonquin ancestors.

LRM -
Lakes Region of Maine, Sebago-Presumpscot Anthropology Project, 2003 (Mawooshen Research)

LRA –

Le Reveil Acadien, (Acadian Cultural Society) August 1995, pages 56-57

LRA MD -

Le Reveil Acadian & Misc. Dictionnaires as referenced. Aug. 2003, pages 68-70 (Acadian Cultural Society)

MA -

"Mi'kmag and Acadian Good Relations," by Website: http://Tucket.com/mikmaq.htm produced by the Yarmouth, Nova Scotia, Congress Mondial Acadien 20004 celebration

MBQ –

Marriage Records of Becancour, Quebec, 1716-1914

MC -

"Metis Culture, 1640-1664," *Canadian History Directory*, 2003, website: http://agt.net/public/dgarneau

METIS –

Metis-L@rootsweb.com Listed on the Internet Message Board Post for Queries and answers http://boards.ancestry.com/mbexec/msg/anChC2ACI/593.1.1

MISC –

Miscellaneous Micmac secondary sources: http://Suttonfamily.biz/abeg10.htm family history; and http://angelfire.com/empire/blaxland/ANCESTOR.html; and http://mywebpage.netscape.com/rjviator/paf/myfamily/pafg22.htm. These sites pertain to Micmac/Lejeune marriage. And Lambert genealogy sources listed at site; Jette; Drouin; LDS; Tanguay, etc. at http://Leveillee.net/ancestry/cadieux1.htm genealogy site.

MNH –
"Metis Nation History, Metis Culture 1763 – 1766," dated 21
Feb. 2003, by website:
http://www.telusplanet.net/public/dgarneau/metis18.htm

MSQ –
Marriage Records of St-Pierre de Sorel, Quebec, 1675-1865

OFCA –
Our French-Canadian Ancestors, 29 Volumes
(Dash after OFCA is the exact volume number material was
found in), by Thomas Laforest. The Lisi Press, P.O. Box 1063,
Palm Harbor, Fl 34682. (They are now out of print.)

PRDH –
"Programme de recherché en demographie historique" from
the University of Montreal, Quebec. (PRDH acte45612;
PRDH individul10948; PRDH famille4552; PRDH
union4552). This location is dedicated to current secondary
sources based on parish registers. This site is very important
dealing with updating sources in question.

PS –
Primary Sources; were Les Familles du Par-de Tousquet
(Genealogy of Wedgeport, Nova Scotia); History et
Genealogy des Acadians by Bona Arsenault; History de Cap-
Sable by Rev. Clarence J. Entremont; listings found on
website:
http://www.geocities.com/swnmetis/html/fam00447.html
dated 20 Jan. 2003

RG –
Roy/LeRoy Genealogy Webpage 2002
http://www.usinternet.com/users/dfnels/roy.htm

TD –

Tanguay (Cyprien), *Dictionaire Genealogy of Families Canadians*, c. 1875, 7 volumes of research in New France and Quebec. (First 2 volumes, 1608-1700, others 1700 and up). Including lists of French married in Female Indian with no dates listed in Vol. 7, page 687, A-C (Material dated 1608-1800)

TG/BM –

From the Tom Glassel and Brenda E. Menard Genealogy Files

TGR – *The Good Regiment*, by Jack Verney, Published 1991 by McQill-Queens University Press

Genocide Attempt Of The Huron

- - - - - - - - - - - - -

The Bear Clan Runs Through My Blood,
As do The Rock People,

From Ontario to Quebec,
We Cried Many Times To Our Fathers,

Why Do Our Brothers Hurt Us So?
A Question For All Humankind.

By Paul J. Bunnell, 2004

OUR ANCESTORS

8AB8LAK
Simon (8ab8lak), died 7 Sept. 1765 au Lac-des-Deux-Montagnes (Grand Chief of the Algonquins, meurt de la picotte). Source – TD

8AB8RA
Marie 8ab8ra, an Abenaquise, born 27 Dec. 1692 at Montreal, Quebec. Source – TD

8ABITTIBY
Charles 8Abittiby, b. 19 Nov. 1683 at Chateau-Richer, Quebec. Source – TD

8AHACHE
Joseph-Marie, baptized 23 March 1760 at la Baie-St-Paul, Quebec, son of Madeleine 8ahache. Source – TD

8AMBIGANICH (SALES) - 8AMBIGANISK8E
Francois De Sales 8Ambiganich married Tarsilie 8Ambriganisk8e. Child was: Francois de Sales, b. 2 Nov. 1686 at Quebec. Source – TD

8AMBOURRA
Francois 8ambourra, an Abenaquis, born 29 June 1698 at Montreal, Quebec. Source – TD

8AN8ASA8ET SAUVAGES
Charles-Louis Sauvages (8an8asa8et), an Abenaquis, baptism 16 Jan. 1701 at Quebec. No marriage listed. Source – TD

8ATANIK
Pierre 8Atanik, an Algonquin, born 19 July 1697 at Montreal, Quebec. Source – TD

8ENTABLA8ET
Jacques (8entabla8et), a Micmac, baptized 18 April 1693 at la Baie-St-Paul, Quebec. No parents or marriage listed.
Source – TD

8NETESIN8
Gabriel 8netesin8, an Algonquin de 2 ans, born 7 Aug. 1697 at Montreal, Quebec. Source – TD

8Ox818mick
Marie 8ox818mick died 14 April 1684 age 4 at Chateau-Richer, Quebec. Source – TD

8SCHI8ANISSE
Marie-Michelle 8Schi8anisse, an Algonquine died 23 Jan. 1686 age 12 at Chateau-Richer, Quebec. Source – TD

8STABANY
Marie-Therese 8Stabany, a Micmac, born 17 Dec. 1690 age 8 at Riviere-Ouelle, Quebec. Source – TD

8TARAMG8AMISKOUE
Marie-Madeleine 8Taramg8amiskoue (Sauvages), an Abenaquise, baptism 1679, death 22 Nov. 1709 at Quebec. No marriage listed. Source – TD

(INDIAN)
Agathe, an Abenaquis Indian died 30 Nov. 1687 at St. Laurent, Quebec. Source – TD

(INDIAN)
Alexandre, an Algonquin, born 2 July 1698 at Montreal, Quebec. Source – TD

(INDIENS/INDIAN)
Alexandre (Indiens), son of Alexandre (Indiens) and Jeanne married Angelique, daughter of Joseph (Indiens) and Suzanne on 2 Feb. 1803 at Becancour, Quebec. Source – MBQ

(INDIAN)
Alexandre, born 6 Oct. 1677 at Boucherville, Quebec. Source – TD

(INDIAN)
Algonquin Indian, born 1615, died 1 April 1695 at Montreal, Quebec. Source – TD

(INDIAN)
Algonquin Indian born 23 May 1695 at Montreal, Quebec. Source – TD

(INDIAN)
Algonquin Indian born 1688, died 9 April 1695 at Montreal, Quebec. Source – TD

(INDIENS/INDIAN)
Amable (Indiens), daughter of Pierre (Indiens) and Marie-Josette married Michel on 17 Sept. 1801 at Becancour, Quebec. Source – MBQ

(INDIAN)
Andre, b. 4 Feb. 1697 at Riviere-Ouelle, Quebec. Source – TD

(INDIAN)
Andre of Lorette, born 2 Feb. 1697 at Beauport, Quebec.
Source – TD

(INDIAN)
Angelique, a Micmac, born 3 Feb. 1691 at Riviere-Ouelle,
Quebec. Source – TD

(INDIAN)
Anne died 16 Feb. 1685 at age 12 at Chateau-Richer, Quebec.
Source – TD

(INDIAN)
Antoine, b. 21 Oct. 1696 at Riviere-Ouelle, Quebec.
Source – TD

(INDIAN)
Antoine, an Abenaquis Indian, b. 3 May 1686 at Chateau-
Richer, Quebec. Source – TD

(INDIAN)
Barbe, an Algonquine Indian, b. 28 April 1670 at Chateau-
Richer, Quebec. Source – TD

(INDIAN)
Barbe, an Algonquine, died 12 July 1698 at Montreal, Quebec.
Source – TD

(INDIAN) (SIOUX)
Barthelemi (Surname possibly Jean?) Listed as an adult of the
Sioux Nation, born 28 Oct. 1687 at Quebec (Baptisted?)
Source – TD

(INDIAN)
Catherine, born 1662, a Montagnaise; died 4 Dec. 1714 at
Chateau-Richer, Quebec. Source – TD

(INDIAN)
Charles, an Algonquin, born 1649, died 23 Oct. 1698 at
Montreal, Quebec. Source – TD

(INDIAN)
Charles, an Algonquin, born 3 June 1697 at Montreal, Quebec.
Source – TD

(INDIAN)
Charles, an Abenaquis Indian, b. 5 Oct. 1693 at Quebec
(Baptism?). Source – TD

(INDIAN)
Claude, born 1695, died 28 April 1696 at Montreal, Quebec.
Source – TD

(INDIAN)
Dominique, a Montagnais Indian died 12 Nov. 1687 at
Beauport, Quebec. Source – TD

(INDIENS/INDIAN)
Dorothee (Indiens), daughter of Jacques-Joseph (Indiens) and
Marie-Elizabeth married Poulin (Indien), son of John-Thomas
Poulin and Marie-Anne Denys 17 Sept. 1805 at Becancour,
Quebec. Source – MBQ

(INDIAN)
Francois-Xavier, an Alganguin, b. 30 Aug. 1687 at Cape de la
Madeleine, Quebec. Source – TD

(INDIAN)
Francois, died 9 July 1692 age 8 at Montreal, Quebec.
Source – TD

(INDIAN)
Francois, born 24 May 1692 at Montreal, age 8, ne a 300 lieues par dela les Illinois, demeurant chez M. Raillot, merchant. Source – TD

(INDIAN)
Francoise, an Algonquine, born 7 June 1695 at Montreal, Quebec. Source – TD

(INDIAN)
Gabriel (Possible last name Jean?), b. 6 August 1687 at Quebec. Source – TD

(INDIAN)
Gabriel, an Algonquin, born 7 May 1697 was age 4 at Montreal, Quebec. Source – TD

(INDIAN)
Genevieve, a savage, born 21 Dec. 1694 age 15. Source – TD

(INDIAN)
Henry-Joseph, et Irois auires Algonquin, born 16 Sept. 1698 at Montreal, Quebec. Source – TD

(INDIAN)
Jacques, an Abenaquis, born 20 Feb. 1690 at Beauport, Quebec. Source – TD

(INDIAN)
Jacques, b. 6 April 1694 at Quebec. Source – TD

(INDIAN)
Jacques, born 9 Nov. 1692 at Cape St. Ignace, Quebec. Source – TD

(INDIAN)
Jacqueline, a Alganquine, died 7 Nov. 1711 at Trois-Rivieres, Quebec at age 112. Source – TD

(INDIAN)
Jacques (Possible last name of Jean), age 12 listed with siblings: Charles-Gabriel age 8; Anne-Josette age 2 months. Source – TD

(INDIAN)
Jean, an Algonquin, born 14 July 1697 at Montreal, Quebec. Source – TD

(INDIAN)
Jean, an Arkansas, born 17 May 1698 and at age 10 was at Montreal, Quebec (following in French) amene de Michillimakina en ce pays en 1697, par Jacques Picard, fils de Hugues Picard, ou il demeura. Source – TD

(INDIAN)
Jean-Baptiste, an Algonquin, born 28 Sept. 1697 at Montreal, Quebec. Source – TD

(INDIAN)
Jean-Baptiste, an Algonquin, died 26 Oct. 1699 age 56 at Montreal, Quebec. Source – TD

(INDIAN)
Jean-Baptiste, an Arkansas, born 21 April 1699 age 9 years at Montreal, Quebec. Source – TD

(INDIAN)
Jean-Baptiste, b. 27 Nov. 1695 at Riviere-Ouelle, Quebec. Source – TD

(INDIAN)
Jean-Baptiste, born 13 Aug. 1687 at Cape de la Madeleine, Quebec. Source – TD

(INDIAN)
Jean-Baptiste, an Algonquin, b. 30 April 1687 at Cape de la Madeleine, Quebec. Source – TD

(INDIAN)
Jean-Baptiste, an Algonquin, born 1648, died 23 Oct. 1698 at Montreal, Quebec. Source – TD

(INDIAN)
Jean, born 14 April 1676 at Sorel, Quebec. Source – TD

(INDIAN)
Jean-Baptiste, born 1692 (appartenant ua Capt. Cote) died 25 March 1709 at St. Thomas. Source – TD

(INDIAN)
Jean-Baptiste, etchemin age 72, born 29 July 1692 at Quebec (Baptism record?) Source TD

(INDIAN)
Jeanne, born 21 July 1698 at Riviere-Ouelle, Quebec. Source – TD

(INDIAN)
Joseph, a Huron of Lorette, Quebec b. 31 May 1691 at Batiscan, Quebec. Source TD

(INDIAN)
Joseph, an Algonquin, born 16 May 1698 at Montreal, Quebec. Source – TD

(INDIAN)
Joseph, a Montagnais Indian, born 4 Dec. 1689 age 2 at St.
Thomas. Source – TD

(INDIAN)
Joseph, born 30 Jan. 1693 (ne de parents payens) age 8 at
l'Ange-Gardien, Quebec. Source – TD

(INDIAN)
Joseph, born 18 May 1695 at Riviere-Ouelle, Quebec.
Source – TD

(INDIAN)
Joseph (frere du precedent) born 18 Aug. 1695 age 6 at
Riviere-Ouelle, Quebec. Source – TD

(INDIAN)
Joseph, Micmac, b. 6 Sept. 1697 at Quebec. Source – TD

(INDIAN)
Joseph-Samuel, an Abenaquis Indian, b. 1678, died 27 Jan.
1703 at Ste. Famille, Quebec. Source – TD

(INDIENS/INDIAN)
Laurent (Indiens), son of Xavier (Indiens) and Angelique
married Marguerite on 15 Sept. 1801 at Becancour, Quebec.
Source – MBQ

(INDIAN)
Louis, born 19 Jan. 1688 at Beauport, Quebec. Source – TD

(INDIAN)
Louis, an Algonquin, b. 13 June 1687 at Cape de la
Madeleine, Quebec. Source – TD

(INDIAN)
Louis, born 13 March 1677 at Sorel, Quebec. Source – TD

(INDIAN)
Louis, a Micmac, born 30 May 1694 at Cape St. Ignace, Quebec. Source – TD

(INDIAN)
Louis, born 2 Oct. 1690 age 3 months. Source – TD

(INDIAN)
Louis, born 6 Oct. 1677 at Boucherville, Quebec. Source – TD

(INDIAN)
Louis, an Arkansas Indian, born 27 Sept. 1696 at l'age de 5 ans, at Ste. Anne de la Perade, Quebec. Source – TD

(INDIAN)
Louis, a Huron Indian, b. 26 Aug. 1678 at Chateau-Richer, Quebec. Source – TD

(INDIAN)
Louis-Medat, born 18 Dec. 1694 at Riviere-Ouelle, Quebec. Source – TD

(INDIAN)
Louise, an Algonquine, born 1 Dec. 1674 at la Pointe-aux-Trembles de Montreal, Quebec. Source – TD

(INDIAN)
Louise, a Montagnaise Indian, born 5 Feb. 1690 age 4 at St. Thomas. Source – TD

(INDIAN)
Louise, a Montagnaise Indian, born 14 Dec. 1687 at Beauport, Quebec. Source – TD

(INDIAN)
Louise-Francoise, a Huron, b. 24 June 1693 at Quebec (Baptism?). Source – TD

(INDIAN)
Lucien (Surname possibly Jean?), enfant savage born 8 Jan. 1688 at Quebec (Baptisted). Source – TD

(INDIAN)
Marguerite, born 15 March 1677 at Sorel, Quebec.
Source – TD

(INDIAN)
Marguerite, born 10 Nov. 1669 at Chateau-Richer, Quebec.
Source – TD

(INDIAN)
Marie, born 14 April 1676 at Sorel, Quebec. Source – TD

(INDIAN)
Marie, born 11 Jan. 1685 at Riviere-Ouelle, Quebec.
Source – TD

(INDIAN)
Marie, born 4 Aug. 1658 at Montreal, Quebec enfant at 10 months, donnee at M. De Maisonneuve, qui l'accepts comme sa propre fille. Source – TD

(INDIAN)
Marie, of the nation of Loups, born Feb. 1681, age de 28 ons; Died 18 Feb. 1681 at Lachine, Quebec. Source – TD

(INDIAN)
Marie, an Abenaquise Indian, born 1673, died 24 Jan. 1688 at Beauport, Quebec. Source – TD

(INDIAN)
Marie-Angelique, an Abenaquise Indian, b. 15 June 1689 (Baptism record). Source – TD

(INDIAN)
Marie-Anne, an Algonquine, born 1688, died 26 Nov. 1698 at Montreal, Quebec. Source – TD

(INDIAN)
Marie-Anne, an Algonquine, born 8 Oct. 1698 at Montreal, Quebec. Source – TD

(INDIAN)
Marie-Anne, born 17 May 1696 at Riviere-Ouelle, Quebec. Source – TD

(INDIAN)
Marie-Francoise, a Micmac, born 20 Jan. 1695 at Cape St. Ignace, Quebec. Source – TD

(INDIAN)
Marie-Francoise, b. 1677, died 9 Nov. 1689 at Beauport, Quebec. Source – TD

(INDIAN)
Marie-Francoise, born 29 Oct. 1698 at Riviere-Ouelle, Quebec. Source – TD

(INDIAN)
Marie-Francoise, a Huron, b. 24 June 1693 at Quebec (Baptism?). Source – TD

(INDIAN)
Marie-Jeanne, an Abenaquise Indian, born 18 Feb. 1691 at
l'Ange-Gardien, Quebec. Source – TD

(INDIAN)
Marie-Josette, a Huron, b. 4 May 1693 at Quebec (Baptism?)
Source – TD

(INDIAN)
Marie-Louise, Micmac, b. 16 June 1697 at Quebec.
Source – TD

(INDIAN)
Marie-Louise, an Acadienne Indian, b. 20 Oct. 1697 at
Quebec. Source – TD

(INDIAN)
Marie-Louise, a Huron, born 29 Feb. 1696 at Montreal,
Quebec. Source – TD

(INDIENS/INDIAN)
Marie-Louise (Indiens), daughter of Louis (Indiens) and Judith
Nemmet married John-Baptiste Metzalabelett 13 Nov. 1883.
Source – MBQ

(INDIAN)
Marie-Madeleine age 31 (Possible baptism, no place or date)
Possible last name of Jean? Source – TD

(INDIAN)
Marie-Madeleine, an Algonquine, born 22 Jan. 1699 at
Montreal, Quebec. Source – TD

(INDIAN)
Marie-Madeleine, a Montagnaise, born 8 April 1692 age one
month. Source – TD

(INDIAN)
Marie-Madeleine, b. 19 Feb. 1699 at Riviere-Ouelle, Quebec.
Source – TD

(INDIAN)
Marie-Madeleine of Acadie, b. 14 Oct. 1692 at Quebec
(Baptism?) Source – TD

(INDIAN
Marguerite-Madeleine, an Abenaquise from Sillery, born 23
Feb. 1687, died 18 Jan. 1688 at Beauport, Quebec.
Source – TD

(INDIAN)
Marie-Marguerite, a Huron from Lorette, Quebec born 15 Jan.
1692 at Charlesbourg. Source – TD

(INDIAN)
Marie-Renee, an Algonquine, died 31 Aug. 1698 at Montreal,
Quebec. Source – TD

(INDIAN)
Marie-Renee, born 30 Aug. 1687 at Cape de la Madeleine,
Quebec. Source – TD

(INDIAN)
Marie-Renee, born 25 May 1695 at Montreal, Quebec.
Source – TD

(INDIAN)
Marie-Ursule of Louise born 20 Dec. 1699. Source – TD

(INDIENS/INDIAN)
Michel (Indiens), son of Joseph-Louis (Indiens) and Josephte
…omis… married Marie-Amable (Indienne) 17 Sept. 1801 at
Becancour, Quebec. Source – MBQ

(INDIAN)
Nipissing, born 28 Aug. 1696, listed as age 3 at Montreal, Quebec. Source – TD

(INDIAN)
Philippe-Richard, born 18 Nov. 1691 at Riviere-Ouelle, Quebec. Source – TD

(INDIAN)
Pierre, an Abenaquis, born 1688, died 28 March 1700 at Montreal, Quebec. Source – TD

(INDIAN)
Rene, born 18 Aug. 1695 age 5 at Riviere-Ouelle, Quebec. Source – TD

(INDIAN)
Romain, born 1687, died 19 Jan. 1688 at Beauport, Quebec. Source – TD

(INDIAN)
Thomas, an Abenaquis, born 1696, died 24 Aug. 1701 at Montreal, Quebec. Source – TD

(INDIAN)
Thomas, born 6 Jan. 1685 at Riviere-Ouelle, Quebec. Source – TD

A8ATANIK
Agathe A8atanik, an Algonquine, born 22 Oct. 1697 at Montreal, Quebec. Source – TD

A8NEM8T
Jeanne (A8nem8t), a Micmac, baptized 18 April 1693 at la Baie-St-Paul. No parents or marriage listed. Source – TD

ACOMO (SAUVAGES)

Francois (Acomo) Sauvages, born 1739, died 8 June 1753 at Quebec. (M. Marcareau, cure, l'avait eleve dapuis l'age de 4 an. Source – TD

AI

Rene Ai, born 14 July 1698 at Montreal, Quebec. Source – TD

ALLARD – LORRAIN (NAGDOTIEOUE)

Francois Allard married Marie Lorrain, daughter of Joseph Lorrain and Cunegonde Nagdotieoue (Illinois woman) at Kaskaskia on 20 Oct. 1726. Francois was the son of Joseph Allard and Marthe Delugre who married at Sainte-Ann du Petit-Cap Quebec on 9 Nov. 1690. (See Lorrain entry below). Source – OFCA XXI

AMENEKIM (SAUVAGES)

Pierre (Sauvages) Amenekim of Loretta, baptism 27 Jan. 1724 at Quebec. Source – TD

AMIOT (METIS) - ?

Daniel Vileneuve Amiot, born 1721 to Daniel-Joseph Amiot and Louise married Madeline ….? Source – BKR

AMIOT-VILLENEUVE – KAPIOUAPNOKOUE & NEPVEUOUIKABE

Born c. 1665 possibly in Quebec. Marie Kapiouapnokoue (Kape8apnok8e/Kape8apnok8e), possibly daughter of … (Outaouaise, Tribe) was the first wife to Daniel-Joseph Villeneuve Amiot who was born 6 Oct. 1665 at Quebec City, Quebec, Canada and died 1726. His parents were, Mathieu Amiot and Marie Miville. Marriage was 2 Sept. 1709 at Montreal, Quebec, Canada. He married again (#2) to Louise Domitilde/Nepveau/Nepveuouikabe/LaFourche (Mackinac) in 1721. She was the daughter of Ke-Wa-No-Quant, born 1707 in

Ottawa, Canada and sister of NisSoWaQuet, also of Ottawa.
Children were: Ann; Marie-Louise; Daniel; Agathe; Canstant.
See: http://www.leveillee.net/ancestry/individu957.htm
  http://www.leveillee.net/ancestry/famille86337.htm
  http://www.leveillee.net/ancestry/famille10471.htm
  http://www.leveillee.net/ancestry/acte47991.htm
  Correction: OUTAOUAIS was her tribe, not her name.
Source – BKR & DNCF & DGA & TD & LEV & PRDH

AMIOT - NEPVEAU/NEPVEUOUIKABE (LaFourche), Louise Domitilde

Louise was the daughter of Ke-Wa-No-Quant, and was born in
1707 in Canada. She was the second wife to Daniel-Joseph
Villeneuve Amiot. They married in 1721. Their children were:
Ann, b. 8 March 1714-15. Died 8 Nov. 1757; Marie Louise
Villeneuve Amiot, b. 10 Jan. 1719-20. Died 1757; Daniel
Vileneuve Amiot, b. 1721; Agathe Langlade/Villenuve Amiot,
b. 5 Sept. 1724, d. 1801; Constant Villeneuve Amiot, b. 1725,
d. 1759. Source – BKR

AMIOT – KITOULAGUE

Jean Baptiste Ambroise Amoit, bourgeois, armurier; born 1694,
son of Jean-Baptiste Amiot and Ambroise married 1715 to Anne-
Marie Kitoulague, a Sauvagesse. He died 16 Aug. 1758 at
Mackinac. (Tanguay says his father was Charles III). Their
children were: Louis, b. 3 Nov. 1740 at Michillimackinac, died
31 Aug. 1760 at Detroit (Michigan); Agnes-Agathe, married 11
Jan. 1751 to Charles Charlu; Francoise, b. 1720, married #1 27
April 1756 to Charles Sauteux, #2 14 Feb. 1757 to Pierre Cario at
Quebec, died 8 Feb. 1760; Marie-Ursule, b. 29 Oct. 1724, died
18 April 1733 at Laprairie; Nicolas, b. 2 May 1730, married 18
Aug. 1755 to Suzanne Sauvage; Marie-Louise, b. 20 March
1732; Marie-Anne, b. 5 April 1734; Ursule, b. 27 Dec. 1738;
Louis, ne le 3 Nov. 1740, born 2 June 1741, died 31 Aug. 1760;
Louis, ne en Dec. 1745, b. 14 June 1746, died 28 Oct. 1757;
Blaise, b.27 Jan. 1749, died 1 Oct. 1750. Source – DNCF & TD

AMIOT (KITOULAGUE LINE) – SAUVAGE
Nicolas Amiot (Amyot), son of Jean-Baptiste Amiot and M.-Anne Kitoulague (Indian) married Suzanne Sauvage 18 Aug. 1755 at Mackinac. Source – DNCF

AMIOT
Thomas Amiot of Lorette, Quebec, baptized 1751, died 13 Sept. 1769 at Lachenaye. No parents listed. Source – TD

ANARAOUI, BARTHELEMY
Barthelemy Anaraqui an Algonquin, but no spouse listed at Trois-Rivieres, Quebec on 16 April 1657. Correction from Léveillée records state that this person was a witness in the wedding of Pierre Couc and Marie Mite8ameg8k8e, not his wedding date. See
http://www.leveillee.net/ancestry/latindocs.htm #mar1657
Copy of primary source PRDH
http://www.leveillee.net/ancestry/acte89036.htm
Correction: The date listed is the date for the marriage of Pierre Couc and Marie Mite8ameg8k8e 16 April 1657. Barthelemy Anar8i was a witness, along with Carolus Pachriini. Jetté incorrectly listed Barthelemy and Carol (Charles) as parents of Mite8ameg8k8e.
Source – JR & LEV & PRDH

ANESCHOM
Etienne (Aneschom), an Amalecite, born 1643, baptized 16 Jan. 1707 at Ste-Anne, Quebec. (A rehabilite son marriage avec Marie, a Micmac, qu'il avait spouse 19 ans auparavant). Source – TD

ANIKOT
Joseph Anikot, an Algonquin, died 19 June 1698 at Montreal, Quebec (The rest in French) avait ete blesse, deux mois aupavant, dans un combat contre les Iroquois. Source – TD

ANNIEHRONNON - DUTCH
Captain Anniehronnon, a Metis son of an Iroquois mother and Dutch father arrived at Quebec in June 1654 from Fort Orange, New Holland (New York) to conclude a peace pact with the natives there. In July 1654 returned to Quebec again with two French prisoners that were captured by the Iroquois. Source – MC

ANTINAEL – SAUVAGESSE
Francois Antinael married Marie, a Sauvagesse. No dated listed (page 16, vol. I). Son was Francois, born 20 Sept. 1784 at Detroit, (Illinois). Source – DNCF & TD

ARDOUIN - LESIEUR
Madeleine Ardouin, an Illinoise (Indian) married Joseph LeSieur after 1700. Source – TD

ARGUINEAU – SAUVAGESSE
Guillaume Arguineau, born 1704 at Riviere-Ouelle, Quebec died 7 July 1749 married Marie Anne who was a Sauvagesse (Indian). Date is not listed but found on page 20 of source. Children were: Gabriel, born 1737, died 20 Dec. 1747; Marie-Angelique, born 17 Feb. 1741, died 26 March 1747; Guillaume, born 24 Nov. 1743. Source – DNCF & TD

ARGUINEAU - ?
Pierre Arguineau whose mother is listed as a Micmac married Genevieve. Her parents are not listed, and there is no marriage date but listing can be found on page of source. Source – DNCF

ARTAUT – MANI8AKIK8CH

Pierre Artaut, Sieur de La Tour (no parents listed) married
Louise Mani8akik8ch a Sauvagesse Algonquine. No marriage
date listed but found on page 23 of source. Tanguay says
married 1670. He was born 1630, she was born 1621. Children
were: Marie, b. 1667 who married 1680 to Michel Des
Rosiers; Jean b. 1676. Source – DNCF & TD

ATONTINON (Iroquoise)

Barbe Atontinon, Iroquoise possibly born 1656, (fille de la
Congregation N.D., died 29 Nov. 1691 at Montreal, Quebec.
There was no spouse listed. Source – TD

ATTINA - SAUVAGESSE

Gabriel Attina married Marie, a Sauvagesse (Indian). Son was
Gabriel, ne 17 Feb. 1783, born 22 July 1786 at Mackinac.
Source – TD

AUBUCHON – PANI8ENSA

Joseph Aubuchon Deszalliers, born 1688, died 1772, son of
Joseph Aubuchon and Elisabeth Cusson married Marie
Pani8ensa, Origins Indienne (Indian) (No parents listed) at
Kaskakia, Quebec on 19 March 1729. Source – DNCF & TD

AYEGABOUCK

Jean-Baptiste Ayegabouck, Micmac age 70, born 2 March
1690 at Quebec (Baptism record?) (Record in French says, par
Manager de St. Valier, filleul de l'intendant Bochart, et de
Dame Reme Damours). Source – TD

BAILLARGEON – CH8PONG8A

Antoine Baillargeon, born 1658, son of Mathurin and Marie
Metayer married #1 to Marie d'Aco and #2 to Domithilde
Ch8pong8a, d'origine Indienne (Indian). Date is not listed but
found on page 41 of source. Children were: Pierre, b. 17 April
1701 at Kaskakia; Marie, b. ets 28 Sept. 1725; Michel, b.

1711, died 3 April 1720 at Montreal, Quebec.
See PRDH
http://www.leveillee.net/ancestry/famille644.htm
http://www.leveillee.net/ancestry/famille8864.htm
http://www.leveillee.net/ancestry/individu6384.htm
Source – DNCF & TD & LEV & PRDH

BARBARAN
Jean-Baptiste Barbaran, a Potocas, affranchi par le R.P.
Grugnas, born 1724, baptism 28 Sept. 1730 at Quebec.
Source – TD

BARON – (ILLINOISE)
Jean-Baptiste Baron (Barron), b. 10 Feb. 1691, son of Leger and
M. Anne Baudon (Daughter of Jacques) married M. Catherine, b.
1703, died 12 Oct. 1745 an Illinoise de Kaskakia (Indian) on 10
Sept. 1749 at Cahokia. Their children were: Joseph; Suzanne who
married #1 12 Oct. 1747 to Jacques Barrois, #2 7 Jan. 1754 to
Joseph Clermont; Marguerite who married 1 July 1754 to Charles
Quesnel, died June 1758; Marie-Catherine, b. 4 et s 15 Dec. 1742.
Jean-Baptiste remarried again 18 Aug. 1748 to Domitilda Rolet at
Cahokia. He died 15 Feb. 1756. Source – DNCF & TD

BARTHELEMI - ABENAQUISE
Mr. Barthelemi married Madeleine Abenaquise (Indian).
Children were: Marie-Joseph, died 29 March 1743 at St-
Antoine Tilly. Source – TD

BATT – CREE WOMAN
Isaac Batt married a Cree Woman. Their daughter Margaret
Nistichio Batt, born c. 1768 at Rupert's Land, died 1829
married c. 1780 at the James Bay area to James Andrew
Spence, born c. 1754 at Howen, Orkney Island, Scotland.
Their son James Spence, b. 1787 at Rupert's Land, died 28
Sept. 1856 at St. Andrew's married Mary (Margaret) Stone
(Indian) 5 Jan. 1830. Source – Metis

BEAUCHAMP - HURON
Barthelemi Beauchamp, son of Jean married 21 July 1749 at Lachenaye to Catherine Huron (Indian), daughter of Athanse. Children were: Marie-Catherine, b. 1 June 1752, married 11 Oct. 1779 to Pierre Laprairie; Barthelemi, b. 3 Dec. 1753; Pierre, b. 30 June 1758; Marie-Catherine, b. 21 Aug. 1759; Jean-Baptiste, b. 19 June 1764; Marie-Judith, b. 6 Dec. 1766. Source – TD

BEDOQUECHETE - PEUPE
Judith Bedoquechete (Sauvagesse) (Indian), spouse of Simon Peupe. Source – TD

BERNARD - INDIAN
Andre Bernard, born c. 1620, France. He died c. 1651. He married twice, #1 to Indian, possibly died 1641. #2 to Marie Andree Guyon c. 1642. She was daughter of Francois Guyon and ...? Andre and Indian wife had following children: Michel Nicolas Bernard was bor c. 1662 who married Margurite (an Indian) who was born 1649, died 1671; Rene Bernard born c. 1663. (Note: This line may need more research). Source – BG

BERNARD – NEPTON
Etienne Nepton (Abenaki Indian), son of Joseph Nepton and Suzanne Louis married Rosalie Bernard 3 Oct. 1854 at Becancour, Quebec. Source – MBQ

BERTRAND (SAUVAGES)
Marie-Louise Bertrand (Sauvages), an Abenaquise, baptism 12 Sept. 1728 at Quebec. No marriage listed. Source – TD

BIGOT – PANIS
Guillaume Bigot married Marie Panis (Indian) Source – TD

BLANCHETIERE – PANIS
Sulpice Blanchetiere married Catherine Panis (Indian).
Source – TD

BLONDIN - INDIAN
Pierre Blondin married an Indian. Children were: Elisabeth, born 21 Jan. 1772 at St-Louis, Missouri. Source – TD

BOISQUIBERT & ROY & LEDUC – AMIOT (METIS)
Agathe Langlade/Villenuve Amiot (Metis), born 5 Sept. 1724 in Michilimackinac, died 1801 in LaBaye, Wisconsin. She married #1, Francois Boisquibert who died 1749; married #2 Amable Roy who died c. 1801 in LaBaye, Wisconsin; married #3 Pierre Leduc-dit-Souligny 21 May 1758 in Michilimakinac, Michigan and died 1764 in LaBaye, Wisconsin.
Source – BKR

BOUCHER – OUEBADDINOUKOUE
Pierre Boucher, born before 1 Aug. 1622 at Montagne, Perche, France, son of Gaspard Boucher and Nicole Lamaine. He was Governor of Trois Riviers, Quebec. He married first to Marie Madeleine (Chretienne) Ouebaddinoukoue, a Huron North American Native on 8 April 1649 at Chambly, Quebec, Canada. Marriage contract was on 17 Jan. 1649. Her parents were not listed. Pierre had the idea of creating a new people by the union of French men and Indian women. The record shows that they had only one child, Jacques Boucher, born c. 1650, but he did not lived long. Marie must have died because Pierre married again to Jeanne Crevier, elder daughter of Christophe Crevier and Jeanne Enard.
PRDH http://www.leveillee.net/ancestry/famille91.htm
http://www.leveillee.net/ancestry/famille602.htm
LEV site http://ww.leveillee.net/ancestry/d307.htm
http://www.leveillee.net/ancestry/individu3300.htm
Article written by Jacques Dunant in *Késsinnimek-Roots-Racines* magazine

Some dates do not correspond! Jacques Dunant's research is current.
Source – OFCA-I & VI & TD & LEV & PRDH

● **BOURASSA - CHEVALIER (MAKINAC)**
Rene Bourassa, June 1718, son of Rene Bourassa, b. 1688 and Agnes Gagne, 1692 married 3 Aug. 1744 to Anne Charlotte Chevalier, a Makinac. Rene died 24 Nov. 1792 at Detroit (Illinois). Source – TD

BOURGERY – ALIMACOUA
Jean-Louis Bourgery, son of Pierre Bourgery and Marie Bouttard married Anne Alimacoua, de Nation Kaskakau (Kascakaon) (Indian) at Detroit (Michigan) on 6 Aug. 1717. Source – DNCF & TD

BRANT U.E. – TEHONAWAGHKWANGERGHKWA
Joseph Brant, a United Empire Loyalist was born March 1742/43 at a Mohawk village near the mouth of the Cuyahoga River, Ohio Territory. He was the fifth child of Peter Tehonawaghkwangerghkwa and Margaret Brant. This family immigrated to the Upper New York area. Joseph's name given at birth was Thayendanegea (pronounced, Tai-yen-da-nay-geh) meaning he who places two bets. Joseph joined the British Army around 1757 at the age of 13 and was noticed by Sir William Johnson. After Johnson's wife died, he married Joseph's sister, Molly Brant. Joseph grew much favor from Johnson after that. He went to Connecticut to learn English, Greek, Latin and Math along with history. He became an Indian translator under Rev. John Stuart. By 1775 he was given the rank of Captain. Johnson had died in 1774. Joseph went to England and was presented at the court of King George III. By 1776 he served with the British as a leader of the Loyalist resistance along with Sir John Johnson (William's

son), Col. Guy Johnson, Col. John Butler and Walter Butler. At the end of the war in 1783, Brant secured a very large land grant for the Six Nations Tribe for their support. This area was near Cataraqui (now Kingston) along the banks of the Grand River (now Brantford. More then 1500 natives settled there. He did much for that new community. He married first to Peggie (Neggan) Margaret in 1765. Their children were: Isaac (1768-1794) married Mary Hill, and Catherine, b.c. 1770 who married Aaron Hill who had child David Hill. Joseph's second wife was Susanna (Margaret, half sister) who died childless; and third wife Catherine Croghan, daughter of George and Catherine Croghan. She died 1838, but gave birth to seven children. Joseph's sister, Molly Brant Johnson is buried at St. Paul's Anglican Church, Kingston, Ontario. Joseph died 24 Nov. 1807, age 65 at his home at Wellington Square on Burlington Bay, Ontario. In 1850 he and his son Capt. John Croghan Brant (1794-1835) were moved from Burlington to The Chapel of the Mohawks at Brantford, Ontario.
Source – JBDF

BRAULT – SAUVAGESSE
Etlienne Brault, Pominville, son of Henry Brault and Claude De Cheurenville married first to Louise Palin, daughter of Mathurin, born 1697, married 8 June 1716, died 27 March 1717, married #2 to Marguerite Sauvagesse (Indian) 15 Oct. 1718 at Rimouski, Quebec. Children were; Pierre, b. 8 April 1719, married 1745 to Therese Paul; Louis-Francois, b. 1 May 1722; Anglique, b. 2 Oct. 1724; Jean-Baptiste, b. 4 Jan. 1727; Gabriel et Claude, b. 12 May 1729; Cecile, b. 25 Aug. 1734, died 11 June 1742 at Montreal, Quebec.
Source – DNCF & TD

BRAULT – PAUL-SAUVAGESSE
Pierre Brault, son of Etienne Brault and Marguerite Sauvagesse (Indian) married Therese Paul-Sauvagesse (Indian) in 1745. Source – DNCF

BREDEL – ST-JEAN-LAVALLEE
Jean Bredel, son of Pierre Bredel and Marie Chagrin of D'Ecrainville, diocese de Rouen, Normandie, France. Jean was a Sergeant in Cie de M. Le Vasseur outfit. He married Madeleine St-Jean-Lavallee, of Nation des Onontagues on 28 April 1696 at Montreal, Quebec. Source – DNCF

BRILLANT – SAUVAGESSE
Jean-Baptiste Brillant married Francoise d'ltagisse-Chretienne (Sauteuse). Source – TD

BROCHET
Alexander Brochet, (Sauvages) appartenant a M. Gline, born 1739, baptized 25 April 1751 at Quebec. No marriage listed. Source – TD

BROCHET
Catherine Brochet, (Sauvagese) appartenant a M. Jacques De la Fontaine, born 1736, baptized 21 July 1748 at Quebec. No marriage listed. Source – TD

BROCHET
Charles Brocket, appartenant au governor, born 1734, baptized 28 Jan. 1747 at Quebec. No marriage listed. Source – TD

BROCHET
Marie-Joseph Brochet, appartenant a Joseph Cadde, baptized 20 April 1747 at Quebec. No marriage listed. Source – TD

BROCHET
Marie-Louise Brochet, appartenant a Jacques De la Fontaine, baptized 20 April 1747 at Quebec. No marriage listed. Source – TD

BRUNET – PANIS
Louis Brunet married Louise Panis (Panic grass).
Source – TD

CADIEU – PEORIAS
Charles Cadieu married Marie-Catherine Peorias (Indian) (Founf in Tanguay, vol. 7). (D. Garneau/Metis genealogy site states: 8 July 1740, Louis Cadeau, Metis son of Charles Cadeau (Cadieu) of Beauport, Quebec, Metis was born at Cahokia, Illinois. Louis mother was Marie Catherine Peorias, born 1728, died 3 July 1758 at Cahokia, Illinois).
Source – TD

CADOT – NIPISSING
Jean-Baptiste Cadot married Anastasie Nipissing, Sauvagesse (Indian) 28 Oct. 1756 at Makinac. Children were: Marie-Renee, nee le 6 Aug. b 15 Oct. 1756; Charlotte, nee le 1 Oct. 1759 au Sault-Ste-Marie, b. 22 May 1760; Jean Baptiste, ne le 25 Oct. 1761, b. 29 June 1762; Michel, b. 30 Aug. 1764.
Source – DNCF & TD

CADOT – NIPISSING
Jean-Baptiste Cadot married to Anastasie Nipissing (Indian).
Source – TD

CADOT – DURAND
Mathurin Cadot (Cadau) Le Poitevin, son of Rene Cadot and Renee Rugande du Poitou married Catherine Durand, daughter of Jean Durand and Catherine Annennontak (Indian) 31 July 1688 at Montreal, Quebec. Source – DNCF

CAIBAS - INDIAN
Barbe, born 1687 and spouse of Richard Caibas died 12 Feb. 1717 at Beauport, Quebec. Source – TD

CALMET – CARIS
Raymond Calmet (Joilibois), son of Antoine Calmet and Antoinette Lacorne of Capel-Bateille, diocese of Cahors, Guyenne, France married Genevieve Caris, Sauvagesse 24 July 1752 at Chambly, Quebec. Source – DNCF

CANASAPIS
Louis Canasapis, born 18 April 1682, died 5 March 1683 at Contrecoeur. Source – TD

CANIBAS
Marie Canibas, baptized 13 Jan. 1731 at Kamouraska, Quebec. No parents listed. Source – TD

CARDINAL – SAUVAGESSE
Jean Cardinal married Marie Sauvagesse (Indian). Date not listed but listed on page 217 of source. Tanguay says child was Catherine, b. 19 Oct. 1772 at Detroit (Michigan). Source – DNCF & TD

CASCARET (SAUVAGES)
Pierre-Louis Sauvages (Cascaret), a Panis of Louisiane. Born 1704, baptism 25 Aug 1718 at Quebec. No marriage listed. Source – TD

CASSIN – LACRIOX
Andre Cassin (Cazin) of Paris, Ile de France married Marie Lacroix, Sauvagesse (Indian) 5 Nov. 1728 at Montreal, Quebec. Source – DNCF

CAUCHERY – ANTAYA
Guillaume Cauchery married M. Josephte Antaya (Possible Indian). Date not listed but is found on page 231 of source. Source – DNCF

CELLIER – (AMERINDIENNE)

Mr. Cellier dit Charet (Memcharet) who died 1708 married c. 1682 in Acadie, Canada to Marie, an Amerindienne who was born around 1663 and died 7 March 1727, Port Royal, Acadie and buried there 8 March 1727. Children were: Jacques, b.c. 1683 married Elisabeth ?; Pierre (the older), b.c. 1687 married #1 Louise Innocent and #2 Francoise Mius, daughter of Philippe & Marie; Pierre (the younger), b.c. 1692 married Madeleine Ouaouamintetces; Marguerite, b.c. 1695. Mr. Cellier, ancestor of the Mi'Kmaq branch of the family could have been the brother of Pierre Cellier, b.c. 1647.
Source – DGDFA, DGDFA Eng Sup, AMD, MNH, LRAMD

CELLIER (CELIER) – SAUVAGESSE

Francois Celier married Marguerite Sauvagesse (Indian). Date not given but listed on page 234 of source. Tanguay says children were: Germain, b. 4 June 1743 at Rimouski; Louis-Francois-Alexandre, b. 28 May 1746. Source – DNCF & TD

CELLIER (DIT CHARET) (AMERINDIENNE) – OUAOUAMINTETCES

Pierre Cellier dit Charet, b.c. 1692, son of Mr. Cellier and Marie (Amerindienne) married 1725 to Madeleine Ouaouamintetces. Source – DGDFA & LRAMD

CHABOT – TAPAKOE

Pierre Chabot was an adventurer and one event would change his life. After entering the village of Kaskaskia in 1708, located on the Illinois River, not too far from Utica he discovered the mission of the Immaculate Conception that was established in 1687. Pierre found his future wife, Symphorose Tapakoe, an Amerindian. Two of their children; Pierre Chabot married Marie-Therese Francoise Lessard. Catherine Chabot married Paul Filion. Other children married at Sainte-Anne du Petit-Cap. After Symphorose died Pierre took a second wife; Dorothee Mercier around 1718. Then moved to Kaskaskia,

They had one child and name him Pierre. Pierre the adventurer passed away on 7 Aug. 1721. His widow remarried to Nicolas Thuillier at Fort de Chartres. Pierre's ancestors (Starting with the oldest first) were; Jean Chabot and Jeanne Rode; Mathurin Chabot, a noble man from Poitou, France. His wife was Marie Mesange, daughter of Robert Mesange and Madeleine Jahan; they had Pierre Chabot. Source – OFCA-XIV

CHARBONNEAU - ?
Frontier Guide, Toussaint Charbonneau, born about 1758, says his mother was a Sioux and father a French Canadian. His wife was a Shoshone, Sacajawea. Was engaged with Northwest Fur Company in 1793 at age 35, trader at Fort Pine on the Assiniboine River, in 1795 left from Lake of the Woods area, moved down to Red River and west to Upper Missouri where he lived. (This source from Tom Bacig 1992 website article). Record says he went on the Lewis and Clark expedition to discover the Pacific Ocean via a mid-continent route. They started out from Saint Louis, Missouri in 1804. The trip was encouraged by president Thomas Jefferson. The record states that Toussaint was from Quebec. There is no listing that this couple had children. Source – OFCA –XXII

CHARLES – DUMAS - ILLINOISE
Jean-Baptiste Charles (Lajeunesse), son of Jean-Baptiste Charles and Madeleine Illinoise (Indian) (His parents are also listed as marrying but not date is listed on page 253 of source) He married Marie-Josephte Dumas, daughter of Joseph Dumas and M. Josephte Ondoyer 20 July 1750 at Montreal, Quebec. Source – DNCF & TD

CHAUVET – PANISE
Pierre Chauvet married to Marie-Madeliene Panise (Indian). Source – TD

CHEGARET
Pierre (Chegaret), baptized 1700, died 13 Jan. 1750 at l'Islet, Quebec. No marriage listed. Source – TD

CHESNE – SAUTEUSE
Antoine Chesne married Marie Jumping Sauteuse (Indian). Source – TD

CHESNE - OUTAOUAISE
Leopold Chesne, son of Charles was born 1734, he was a Captain, and died 13 Jan. 1778 at Detroit. He married c. 1774 to Marie Outaouaise (possible Indian). Children were, Charles, b. 25 Oct. 1775; Catherine, b. 12 May 1776. Source – TD

CHEVALIER – KINII8ENA
Amable Chevalier (Sauvage) (Indian) married Catherine Kinii8ena, Sauvangesse (Indian). Date not given but listed on page 268 of source. Children were: Marie, baptism 15 Aug. 1787 at Mackinac; Marie-Louise, Baptism 1 Sept. 1789. Source – DNCF & TD

CHEVALIER – SAUVAGESSE
Bathelemi Chevalier married a Marie Sauvagesse (Indian). Date not given but listed on page 268 of source. Child was, Marguerite, nee 1784, Baptism 22 Jult 1786 at Mackinac. Source DNCF & TD

CHEVALIER – SAUVAGESSE
Luc Chevalier, b. 1735, son of Jean-Baptiste Chevalier and Francoise Alavoine married a Marie Sauvagesse (Indian). Date not given but listed on page 270 of source. Children were: Marguerite, nee 23 Dec. 1778 at Mackinac, born 20 July 1786; Joseph, ne 17 April 1782, born 20 July 1786; Jean-Baptiste, ne 4 Feb. 1785, b. 20 July 1786 (births may be Baptisms?) Source – DNCF & TD

CHEVERY – SAUVAGESSE

Dominique Chevery married a Marie Sauvagesse (Indian). Not date given but listed on page 272 of source. Children were: Madeleine, nee 17 March 1782, baptism 13 Aug. 1786 at Mackinac; Etienne, ne 5 Feb. 1785, baptism 13 Aug. 1786. Source – DNCF & TD

CHICACHATS

Marie-Joseph Chicachats, appartenant au Chevalier de Longueuil, born 1729, baptized 30 Jan. 1753 at Quebec. No marriage listed. Source – TD

CLAUDE (AMERINDIAN MI'KMAQ?)

Jean Claude married Marie Salle. In Stephen White's book he finds that Father Clarence d'Entremont supposed Jean Claude was an Amerindian Mi'kmaq but there is no documentation to prove this. A Father Patrice Gallant wondered if he may be in fact Jean-Claude Landry because Marie Salle lived all around the Landry's during the census of 1686. This case still needs work. Source – DGDFA Eng Sup

CLAUDELE

Joseph Claudele, Tele-de-Boule married Marguerite ?, an Algonquinne, veuve de Jacques Abenaquis on 25 Feb. 1779 at Ste-Anne-de-la-Perade, Quebec. Source – TD

CLUSEAU – PELLETIER

Pierre Cluseau (Loranger), son of Jean-Baptiste Cluseau and Anne Jamien married Marie Pelletier daughter of Nicolas Pelletier and Marie Sauvagesse (Indian) 24 Sept. 1731 at Quebec. Source – DNCF

COCHERY – AUBERT
Charles Cochery, Cocheri dit St-Onge, son of Guillaume
Cochery and M. Josephte Pelletier-Antaya (Possible Indian)
married Francoise Aubert, daughter of Marcellin Aubert and
M. Therese Metot 5 July 1773 at Quebec. Source – DNCF

COCHERY – PELLETIER-ANTAYA
Jean-Baptiste-Guillaume Cochery de Saintonge married M.
Josephte Pelletier-Antaya (Possible Indian), daughter of
Michel Pelletier-Antaya (Possible Indian) and Francoise
Meneux 30 July 1737 (Contract Notary P.A. De La Fosse).
Source – DNCF

COTE (or BOTTE dit SORAK8A) – A8ENDEA
Abraham Cote (or Botte) dit Sorak8a came from St-Jacques,
Dieppe, Normandie, France, son of Abraham Cote and
Jacqueline Caille. He married at mountain Indian Mission at
Montreal, Quebec on 14 Oct. 1680. Her name was Onondaga
Marie A8enda, an Onontaise (Indian). There is some question
whether Abraham was really a Cote because his children were
baptished under the names of Botte or Sorak8a. It is possible
they were assimilated into the Indian culture and lost their real
name. Tanguay says children were: Jacques, b. 7 Feb. 1685;
Jeanne, b. 10 Feb. 1688; Jean Baptiste, b. 26 Nov. 1689;
Simon, b. 5 Jan. 1699. Source – OFCA – VI & DNCF & TD

COTTENOIR(E) – 8AQK8AT
Jean-Baptiste Cottenior, son of Louis Cottenior and Angelique
Desrosiers married Marie Josephte 8aqk8at (Sauvangesse) in
1759. Child was: Marie, nee 1 Nov. 1759, baptism 16 July
1760 at Mackinac. Source – DNCF & TD

COUC – LAFLEUR – MONTOUR LINES

The Following Couc family has had much added or corrected based on Norm Léveillée, Suzanne Boivin Sommerville, and PRDH research and documents found in primary and secondary sources. Websites to be consulted for expanded materials are: http://ww.leveillee.net/roots/suzanne8.htm (Suzanne Boivin Sommerville's arcticle on Kessinnimek-Roots-Racines).

At these sites there are several articles and stories by the authors on the Couc-Montour families. Jette had committed several errors in regards to Marie Mite8ameg8k8e, the eighth great-grandmother of Norm Léveillée. His own story on her can be found at http://www.leveille.net/ancestry/mariem.htm based on all the documentation hs found. I have left the other source findings listed here, but the most recent findings by the above researchers must be considered and added.
Source – LEV & PRDH

COUC – MITEOUAMIGOUKOUE, MARIE

Corrected Entry by Léveillée Records
Pierre Couc dit Lafleur, born c. 1624 (PDRH records say 1627), Cognac, Saintes, Saintonge, (Xaintes, Xaintonge) Charente, France. Was a soldier and interepreter at Trois-Rivieres, Quebec on 24 Aug. 1651. He was also a farmer Léveillée records stated Tanguay or Jette sources had an error in translation date 6 Aug. 1665 as Pierre's death where it really was the date he was wounded. His actual death was 5 April 1690 at St-Francois-du-Lac, Quebec so the above date was not that of a son. It was said that many people turned out for his funeral. (See Léveillée's site for details at http://www.leveille.net/ancestry/d294.htm)
Pierre married Marie Mite8ameg8k8e (An Algonquine) on 16 April 1657 at Trois-Rivieres, Quebec.
Their children were: Jeanne, b. 14 July 1657 at Trois-Rivieres, Quebec, died 23 Oct. 1679; Louis (dit Montour), baptized 27 Nov. 1659 at Troi-Rivieres, First married 1681 to Madeleine

Sacokie, Children were, Francois (dit Montour), b. 4 June
1681, Sorel, Quebec, died 9 Dec. 1700, Trois-Rivieres, and
Jacques (Jean Montour), baptized 5 Jan. 1684 at Trois-
Rivieres. Then second marriage on 7 Jan. 1688 at St-Francois-
du-Lac, Quebec to Jeanne Quigetigoucoue (Native). Louis
died Spring, 1709 killed while bringing western Indians to
trade at Albany (NY); Their children were: Marie Angelique,
b. before 1662 at Cap-de-la-Madeleine, Quebec, Married 30
Aug. 1682 in Sorel, Quebec to Francois (Delpe) Delpestcerny
(St-Cerny/St-Sorny/St-Serny). Marie died 7 Oct. 1750, Pointe-
du-Lac, Quebec; Marguerite, b. 1 June 1664, Trois-Rivieres,
married before 31 Dec. 1686 to Jean Fafard; Isabelle Elisabeth
Marie, b. before 1667 Lieu indetermine (au Quebec), First
married 30 April 1684 at Sorel, Quebec to Joachim Germanau.
Isabelle died 1752, in the English Colonies; Marie Madeleine,
b. before 1669, Quebec, Married 31 Dec. 1684 to Maurice
Menard Fontaine; Jean, b. before 1673, Quebec, married
before 24 Nov. 1706 to Anne ?
Marie Mite8ameg8k8e was married first to Assababich (b.c.
1620) c. 1645 and had two children: Catherine, b. 1647,
baptized 1 Nov. 1652 at Trois-Riviers, Quebec; Pierre,
baptized 6 May 1650.
Source – LEV & PRDH

COUC – QUIGESIAG8K8E
Louis Couc (Montour), son of Pierre Couc and Marie
Mite8ameg8k8e (Indian) married Jeanne Quigesiag8k8e, an
Algonquine 7 Jan. 1688 at St. Francois du Lac, Quebec. Also
married Madeleine Sacokie 1681. Source – DNCF & TD

COURCAMBEC – DENIAU
Pierre Courcambec (Courcaubec) married Rose Deniau,
daughter of Rene Deniau and Anastasie, of the Illinois Nation
7 Feb. 1727 at Detroit, Michigan. Source – DNCF

COURCHENE – LAFOND

Jean-Baptiste Courchene (Brisset), sauvage (Indian) of the Kiakionnas Nation married Marguerite Lafond (born 1685), daughter of Jean Lafond and Catherine Senecal 13 Jan. 1710 at Batiscan, Quebec. They had 8 children.
Source – DNCF & DGA

COUTURNIER – ANNENNONTAK

Jacques Couturnier (Dressmaker), son of Jean Couturnier and Marie Aumont of Gonneville-sur-Mer, pres de Caen, Normandie, France married Catherine Annennontak, (Huronne) daughter of Nicolas Annennontak and Jeanne Obrih8andet both Huron Indian on 28 Nov. 1672 (Contract by Notary Rageot). (veuve de Jean Durand). Son was Denis Joseph Couturier (Metis), born 11 Jan. 1712, Becancour (Batiscan), Quebec. Tanguay says, Jacques born 1646, (etabli au Carouge) and Catherine, born 1649 (veuve de Jean Durand). Children were: Charles, 1 March 1673 at Quebec, died 25 April 1699 at Batiscan, Quebec; Jacques, b. 11 Feb. 1675; Genevieve, b. 28 March 1679 at Sillery, Quebec died 24 March 1715 and married 31 Oct. 1701 to Jean Metivier; Denis-Joseph, b. 20 March 1681 at Lorette, Quebec and first married 11 Jan. 1712 to Catherine Proteau and married second 21 Feb. 1718 to Angelique Tellier at Cape Sante, Quebec; Catherine, born 17 April 1687, died 25 May 1687. Third marriage was 13 April 1733 to Therese Hamel at Deschambault, Quebec. Source – DNCF & DGA & DT

COUTURNIER – HAMEL – PROTEAU – LE TELLIER

Denis-Joseph Couturnier, son of Jacques Couturnier and Catherine Annennontak (Indian) married Therese Hamel, daughter of Jean-Francois Hamel and Felicite Levasseur 13 April 1733 at Deschambault. He is listed again with marriage to Catherine Proteau, daughter of Luc Proteau and M. Madeleine Germain 11 Jan. 1712 at Batiscan. He has a 3rd. marriage to Angelique Le Tellier, daughter of Francois Le

Tellier and Anne Page 21 Feb. 1718 at Cap Sante, Quebec.
Source – DNCF

COUVRET – SAUTEUSE
Joseph Couvret married Charlotte Jumping Sauteuse (Indian).
Source – TD

CRISTINAUX, ANTOINE
Born 1727, baptized 22 Dec. 1743 at Quebec. No marriage
listed. Source – TD

CRISTINAUX
Jean-Francois, Cristinaux, appartenant a M. Duburon, born
1728, baptized 22 Dec. 1743 at Quebec. Died 20 Feb. 1744.
Source – TD

CUILLERIER – PADOKA
Rene-Hilaire Cuillerier, son of Rene Cuillerier and Marie
Lucault married Elisabeth Padoka (Indian.) Date not listed but
on page 328 of source. Source – DNCF & TD

D'ABBADIE - DAMOUR
Bernard Anselme d'Abbadie de Saint Castin (1689-1720)
(Metis) married Marie Charlotte Damour c. 1712. Had a
female daughter born in Quebec 1712. Source – DGA

D'ABBADIE – MADOKAWANDO
Jean-Vincent D'Abbadie born 1652, died 1708, son of Jean-
Jacques (D'Abbadie) St. Castin and Isabeau (DeBearn)
Bonasse married Marie Pidicwammiskwa Madokawando 1670
at Acadie, Canada, daughter of Chief Madokawando and his
Indian wife in 1685. Their children were: Therese
(D'Abbadie) St. Castin and Infant St. Castin. (I am not sure
why last name changed to St. Castin?). This record also says
Jean married Mathide, daughter of the same family on the
same date? (Possible error in names or he married both

sisters?). Their children were: Claire; (Mr. Chateauneuf (Meneux) D'Abbadie; Philippe Meneux D'Abbadie; Anastasie; Bernard; Bernard-Anseline; Jean-Pierre; Ursuline; Joseph; Barenos (St. Castin) D'Abbadie. Source – AMD

D'ANTICOSTI
Louise-Claire d'Anticosti, appartenant a M. De Fleury, Lagorgendiere, born 1731, baptized 9 Aug. 1735 at Quebec. No marriage listed. Source – TD

D'ANTIGONISH
Gilette d'Antigonish, baptized 21 June 1746 at Quebec. No marriage listed. Source – TD

D'ASSINIBOINE
Christine d'Assinihoine, appartenant a Nicolas Jacquin, born 1726, baptized 19 April 1739 at Quebec. No marriage listed. Source – TD

DARPENTIGNY – SAUVAGESSE
Jean-Baptiste Darpentigny married Madeleine-Therese Sauvagesse (Indian) 1685. Tanguay says they had a child, Francoise, b. 8 Feb. 1686 at Montreal, Quebec. Source – DNCF & TD

DAUNET – SAUVAGESSE
Antoine Daunet married a Marie Sauvagesse. No date given but listed on page 343 of source. Children were: Antoine, ne 1779, baptism 7 July 1785 at Detroit (Michigan); Therese, nee 1782, baptism 7 July 1785. Source – DNCF & TD

DE8ATIC
Philippe (De8atic), an Algonquin, baptized 1677, died 2 April 1737 at St-Francois, I. J. Parents no listed. Source – TD

DEGRE/DEGREZ – AMERINDIAN
Michel Degre/Degrez is listed with an Ameridian wife on grand dated 3 Aug. 1689 at Pokemouche getting a league of frontage on the river Pokemouche in the Bay of Chaleurs, Quebec, Miscou coast, 25 leagues from Ile Percee, and the right to trade with the Indians, and hunt and fish. Source – DGDFA Eng Sup

DELAUNAY – R8ECANGA
Louis Delaunay (Paquier-Pinguet), born 1650, son of Pierre Delaunay and Francoise Pinguet married Marie Catherine R8ecanga (Sauvagesse)1694. Children were: Jean-Jacob, baptism 25 July 1695 at Kaskakia, Quebec; Charles, baptism 29 May 1698. Source – DNCF & TD

DEMITTE – D'ANTAYA
Francoise DeMitte married Marie-Louise d'Antaya (Indian). Source – TD

DENIS – BERTAU/BERTRAND/AMERINDEINNE
Jean Denis, Baptisted 4 Feb. 1674 at Point Aux Tremble, Portbeuf, Quebec, son of Jean Denis and Genevieve Billau/Billot. He died 1729 in Acadia, Canada. He married Cecile Bertrand (Amerindienne) Bertau in 1703 in Acadia. Children were: Marie-Anne, Marie-Louise, Marie. Source – MNH & LERAMD

DENIS – SAUVAGES
Marie-Marguerite, baptized 9 Jan. 1776 at l'Islet, Quebec, daughter of Germain-Urbain and Marie Denis, both Micmacs. Source – TD

DENIS – SAUVAGESSE
Nicolas Denis (Sieur De Fronsac), son of Richard Denis and Anne Parabego married Marie Sauvagesse (Indian). No date given but listed on page 381 of source. PRDH

http://ww.leveillee.net/ancestry/famille8763.htm
http://ww.leveillee.net/ancestry/individu75752.htm
Source – DNCF & TD & LEV & PRDH

DENYS – (AMERINDIENNE)
Nicolas Denys dit Fronsac, b.c. 1682 at Beaumont, Acadie,
buried 3 Feb. 1732, Beaumont, Quebec, son of Richard Denys
and Anne Patarabego (Indian) married 1707 in Acadie to
Marie, an Amerindienne. Children were: Marie, b.c. 1702
married Michel Masson; Francois, b.c. 1708; Gabriel, b.c.
1716; Jacques, b.c. 1717.
http://www.leveillee.net/ancestry/cadieux.htm
PRDH: http://www.leveillee.net/ancestry/famille87643.htm
Source – DGDFA & AMD & LEV & PRDH

DENYS – (INDIENS)
Marie-Anne Denys married Pierre (Indiens), son of Pierre
(Indiens) and Marie Jibois 9 Nov. 1852 at Becancour, Quebec.
Source – MBQ

DENYS – (INDIEN)
Marguerite Denys, daughter of John-Baptiste Denys married
Laurent (Indien) 15 Sept. 1801 at Becancour, Quebec.
Source – MBQ

DENYS – METZALABALETT
David Denys (Indian line), son of Jacques Denys and
Madeleine Francois married Marie Metzalabalett 20 Jan. 1876
at Becancour, Quebec. Source – MBQ

DENYS/DENIS – PATARABEGO/PARABEGO

Richard Denis married Anne Parabego (Indian).
Richard Denys de Fransac, son of Nicolas Denys and
Marguerite de Lafitte married 1680 to Anne Patarabego an
Amerindienne. Son, Nicolas listed above. And a daughter
Marie-Anne Denys de Fronsac, born 1681, Beaubassin,
Acadie, Canada, died 9 Oct. 1728 at Montreal, Quebec. She
married Jean (LaPierre) Mercan (1685-1718), son of Pierre
Mercan and Francoise Baiselat on 16 Oct. 1709, Quebec,
Quebec.
There are three files on the following site that will verify and
maybe add information.
PRDH http://ww.leveillee.net/ancestry/union87640.htm
http://ww.leveillee.net/ancestry/individu21580.htm
LEV http://ww.leveillee.net/ancestry/cadieux.htm
Source – DGDFA & MNH & DGA & LEV TD & PRDH

DESROSIERS – ARTAUT

Michel Desrosiers, son of Antoine Desrosiers and Anne Du
Herisson married M. Jeanne Artaut, daughter of Pierre Artaut
and Louise Manit8kik8ch 14 Jan. 1679 (Contract Notray by
Audouard. Source – DNCF

DE ST. CASTIN – PIDIE8ANMISK8E

Vincent De St. Castin Baron de St. Castin (Sieur) was born in
St. Castin, France. Parents not listed. He married Marie
Pidie8anmisk8e (Dame) (no date) (No parents listed. Theyu
had a daughter, Theresa Se St. Castin (De Pobomkou). She
married Philippe Mius on 4 Dec. 1707. Source – OFCA-XXII

DE ST-ETIENNE – MICMAC

Charles-Amador De St-Etienne (De La Tour), son of Claude
De St-Etienne of France married a Micmac girl in 1626.
Source – DNCF

DICAIRE – VISSE-RIZ

Pierre Dicaire (Dickerre), son of Louis Dicaire and M.
Suzanne Lorain married Cecile Visse-Riz, daughter of Julien
Visse-Riz and M. Angelique Iroquoise 7 Feb. 1743 at Lac des
Deux-Montagnes, Quebec. Source – DNCF

DIMENSIONED/BOTTE (SORAKA) - A8ENDEA (ONONTAISE)

Abraham Dimensioned or Botte (says Soraka) was husband of
Marie A8endea (Onontaise). Source – TD

DORION – PADOKA

Joseph Dorion married Marie-Anne Padoka (Indian), veuve de
Louis Picard. Source on page 687. Source – TD

DOUAIRE - TAMANIKOUE

Charles Douaire married Marie Tamanikoue (Indian). Child
was Catherine, Baptism 1 Feb. 1727 at Bout-de-Ille, M.,
Quebec. Source on page 687. Source – TD

DOUCET – (AMERINDIEN?)

Germain Doucet married Francoise around 1708 de la riviere du
Port Royal. The word "Amerindien" is a reference that is
probably Francoise descent. No children listed. But in the AMD
source it says Germain (Amerindienne) Doucet and his wife
was Francoise, but note from Stephen A. White translation;
Father Archange Godbout, Germain's family appears in the
1708 census under the name of Medosset. Possible conflict in
documentation because in this census it says Germain's wife is
called Marie-Charlotte, but in parish records it says Francoise.
In the 1708 Port Royal Census lists this family as Medosset.
There is one child listed as Francois Doucet born 1709 who
married 25 June 1726 to Marie Pisnet at Port Royal, Acadie.
She was born 1707 to Pierre (Amerindienne) Pisnet and Anne.
Ref. http://www.leveillee.net/ancestry/d264.htm
Source – DGDFA & AMD & LRAMD & LEV

DOYON – (INDIAN SLAVE)

Nicolas Doyon (1654-1715), son of Jean Doyon and Marthe Gagnon married Genevieve Guyon in 1690. He was a famous gunsmith and arquebusier who went to Illinois in 1683. While there he married an Indian slave. They had a son born in 1684 who later became a blacksmith in Boucherville, Quebec. Check out the documents at
http://www.leveillee.net/ancestry/d567.htm
PRDH http://www.leveillee.net/ancestry/famille662.htm
And any links from these pages.
PRDH
http://www.leveillee.net/ancestry/actes/famille6496.htm
The data contained therein doesn't seem to support the information about going to Illinois in 1683. Take a look at the children and the year of their birth! What was LaForest's source for this information?
Source – OFCA, VII & LEV & PRDH

DRESSMAKER – ANNENNONTAK

Jacques Dressmaker was the second husband to Catherine Annennontak (Huron), widow of Jean Durand. Source – TD

DROUET – SAUVAGESSE

Joseph Drouet (Sieur De Richerville), born 16 March 1711, Detroit married a Marie Sauvagesse (Miamis Indian). Source found on TD page 687. Date not given but listed on page 422 of source. Children were, Joseph; Jean-Baptiste; Charlotte et Anne, baptism 14 March 1773 at Detroit (Michigan).
Source – DNCF & DGA & TD

DUBEAU (DU BOC) (DUBOUQ) – HARNOIS

Guillaume Du Boc (Dubocq), son of Laurent Dubeau and M. Felix Arontio (Huron Indian) was a Captain in the militia married Marguerite Harnois, daughter of Isaac Harnois and Marguerite Blaise 22 Nov. 1703 at St. Augustin, Quebec.
Source – DNCF

DUBEAU/DUBOCQ – HARBOIS

Jean Dubeau (1669- 12 Sept.1743), son of Laurent Dubeau and M. Felix Arontio (Huron Indian) married Marguerite Harnois (1677- 20 May 1747), daughter of Isaac Harnois and Marguerite Blaise 22 Nov. 1703 at St. Augustin, Quebec. Children were: Marguerite-Louise, baptism, 9 July 1704 at Ste-Foye, married 20 Oct. 1722 to Antoine LeMarie; Marie-Joseph, baptism 5 April 1706, died 8 Dec. 1729 at Quebec Jeanne Dubeau/Dubocq (Metis), born 11 Jan. 1709 Ste Foye, Quebec, died 30 Sept. 1713, Marie Jeanne, b. 1710 who married Jean Francois Chantal 4 Aug. 1734, St. Augustin; Joseph-Charles, baptism 8 March 1712 at Lorette, Quebec, died 30 Sept. 1713; Marie-Francoise, baptism 24 Feb. 1715, married 19 April 1736 to Jean-Baptiste Valieres; Marie-Charles, baptism 25 April 1717, died 3 May 1740; Joseph, married 1753 to Marie-Louise Petit.
Source – DNCF & DGA & TD

DUBEAU (DUBOCT) – ARONTIO

Laurent Dubeau (Duboct), son of Jacques Dubeau and Elisabeth Pruneau of St. Maclou de Rouen, Normandie, France married M. Felix Arontio, Huron (Huronne) (Source TD page 687) Native on 19 Sept. 1662 at Quebec. Tanguay says Laurent was born 1636, son of Jacques Du Bocq and Elizabeth Pruneau of St. Maclon de Rouen, France. Laurent married Marie-Felix Arontio, a Huronne Indian, daughter of Joachim Arontio of La Conception, Ontario, a Huron. She died 1 Nov. 1689 at Montreal. Children were: Joseph, b. 24 June 1666; Jean, b. 10 June 1669, Married 22 Nov. 1703 to Marguerite Harnois at St-Augustin, died 12 Sept. 1743; Jean-Baptiste, baptism 13 Aug. 1707, married Marie Lamotte; Laurent, 3 Feb. 1672 who married #1 23 Sept. 1697 to Francoise-Paule Campagna at St. Augustin, Quebec and #2 10 Sept. 1718 to Marie-Francoise Sevigny, died 15 July 1731; Philippe, b. 29 Oct. 1675; Marie-Anne, b. 28 August 1678 at Sillery and became an ursuline named Ste. Marie Madeleine who died 20 August 1734; Louise Catherine, b. 22 June 1681 who married 6 May 1700 to Jean Ride. Source – DNCF & TD

DUBEAU – CAMPAGNA
Laurent Dubeau (Du Bau), born 22 Aug. 1700, at St. Augustin, Quebec, son of Laurent Dubeau (1672 - 1731) and M. Felix Arontio (Huron Indian) married Francoise Paule Campagna (1683-1717), daughter of Pierre Campagna and Francoise-Anne Martin 23 Sept. 1697 at St. Augustin, Quebec. He marry's again to Marie Sevigny, daughter of Julien-Charles Sevigny and Marguerite Rognon (Voir De Sevigne) 10 Sept. 1718 at St. Augustin, Quebec. Laurent and Francoise had another son, Jacques, born 13 Feb. 1708, Quebec, Quebec, and Joseph Marie, born 27 March 1710, Lorette, Quebec who married Madeleine Gaboury 27 Aug. 1731, St. Augustin, Quebec. Source – DNCF & DGA

DUBOIS (SAUVAGE) - CAMPAGNA
Michel Dubois (Sauvage) married 8 Jan. 1757 at St-Frs-du-Luc to Marie-Joseph Campagna, daughter of Jean-Baptiste, born 1736. Children were: Marie-Joseph, baptism 7 Aug. 1757, died 4 Jan. 1758; Michel, baptism 16 Dec. 1758, died 28 April 1760 at St-Laurent, M., Quebec. Source – TD

DUCHESNE – (AMERINDIAN ORIGIN – PANIS NATION)
Andre Duchesne dit Leroide was listed as Amerindian origin of the Panis Nation married M. Anne Groinier on 2 Oct. 1719 at Quebec. She was the daughter of Nicolas Groinier and Anne Chretien. They had four daughters, three of whom were born at Beaumont, Quebec. Source – OFCA – XI & DNCF

DULIGNON - LEMAIRE (SAUVAGESSE)
Jean DuLignon, son of Pierre, died avant 1762 married 30 Sept. 1737 at Michillimackinac to Marie-Joseph-Angelque (Sauvagesse) died avant 1762. Children were: Louis-Josue, born 1734, baptism 17 Oct. 1736, married 23 Nov. 1750 to

Elisabeth Lacroix at St-Michel, Quebec; Marie-Therese, born 19 Nov. 1738, baptism 14 July 1739, married 31 Aug. 1762 to Joseph-Laurent Berthand at Montreal; Angelique, baptism 19 May 1740; Paul, born 31 Oct. 1742 at Sault-Ste-Marie, baptism 1July 1743; Francoise-Marie-Anne, baptism 5 Aug. 1744; Marguerite-Joseph, baptism 17 June 1747. Source – TD

DUMOUCHEL – SAUVAGESSE
Louis Dumouchel, son of Bernard Dumouchel and M. Anne Tessier married Francoise Sauvagesse (Indian) 1769.
Source – DNCF

DUMOUCHEL - SAUVAGESSE
Louis Dumouchel, son of Bernard, baptism 1725 married 1769 to Francoise Sauvagesse (Indian). Children were: Bernard, born 22 March 1770, baptism 9 July 1775 at Mackinac; Jean, born 12 Jan. 1772, baptism July 1775; Francoise, born 12 May 1774, baptism July 1775, married #1 to Pierre Ducheneau, #2, 1 Nov. 1795 to Antoine Grandbois at Cahokia; Joachim, born June 1776, baptism 22 July 1786; Marie-Joseph, born 26 Dec. 1778, baptism 22 July 1786, married 28 Nov. 1793 to Louis Labossiere; Madeleine, born 17 Aug. 1784, baptism 22 July 1786. Source – TD

DUQUET – SAUVAGESSE
Pierre Duquet married a Sauvagesse (Indian). No date given but listed on page 464 of source. Child was, Pierre, baptism 1717, died 19 April 1760 at Ste-Famile, Quebec. Source – DNCF & TD

DUQUET – SAUVAGESSE
Pierre Duquet married Marie Sauvagesse (Indian) (Source page 687). Source – TD

DURAND – ANENONTHA/ANNENNONTA

Jean Durand dit Lafortune, born 1640, son of Louis Durand and Madeleine Malvande of Doeuil-sur-le-Mignon, diocese of Saintes, Saintonge, France married Catherine Anenontha or Annennontak, a Huron, (Huronne, source page 687) born 1649, daughter of Nicolas Annennontak (Arendankir) and Jeanne Obrih8andet, both Huron after 12 Feb. 1663 when a first marriage contract with Marie Fayet was canceled. Marriage date was 26 Sept. 1662 at Quebec. Tanguay says Jean was born 1640, son of Louis Durand and Madeleine Malvande of Deuil, eveche of Xaintes. Jean died 1671. He married 26 Sept. 1662, Quebec to Catherine Axnennontak a Huron b. 1649. She fled the Georgian Bay (Ontario) area after her father was killed in 1658. Children were: Louis, baptism 14 Nov. 1670 at Sillery, Quebec, married #1 9 Sept. 1698 to Elisabeth-Agnes Michel, #2, 30 Jan. 1719 to Jeanne Houde at St-Nicolas, Quebec. Marie, b. 21 April 1666 who married 31 July 1688 to Mathurin Cadau; Ignace, b. 1669 who married 24 Feb. 1691 to Catherine Miville and died 30 Nov. 1697 at Cap St. Ignace; Louis, b. 14 Nov. 1670 at Sillery, Quebec who married 9 Sept. 1698 to Elizabeth Agnes Michel.
Source – OFCA – XXIX & DNCF & TD

DURAND – HOUDE

Louis Durand, son of Jean Durand and Jeanne (Record does say Jeanne, not Catherine?) Annennontak married Jeanne Houde, daughter of Jean Houde and Anne Rouleau 30 Jan. 1719 at St. Nicolas. There is another married to Elisabeth Michel, daughter of Olivier Michel and Madeleine Cochon 9 Sept. 1698 at Quebec. Source – DNCF

DURAND - MICHEL

Louis Durand, Metis, born 1670 married Elisabeth Agnes Michel dit Taillon (born 1682, died 1718) They had a son, Louis born 13 Aug. 1700 at Quebec City, Quebec, married Marie Anne Dumay on 22 Jan. 1725 at Sorel, Quebec. They had a daughter, Elisabeth (Metis), born 26 March 1708 at St. Antoine-Tilly, Quebec who married Andre Lacoste 10 April 1736 at Montreal, Quebec, Daughter Genevieve (Metis), born 25 Dec. 1709, St. Nicolas, Quebec, died 21 Jan. 1710 at same place, daughter Marie Charlotte (Metis) born 3 April 1711, St. Nicolas, Quebec. Source – DGA

DURAND – MIVILLE
Ignace Durand (Durant), son of Jean Durand and Catherine Annenontak (Indian) married M. Catherine Miville, daughter of Jacques Miville and Catherine Baillion 24 Feb. 1691 at Quebec. Source – DNCF

ENAULT – AMERINDIENNE MICMAC
Philippe Enault de Barbaucannes was born c. 1651. He married an unnamed Ameridienne Micmac in 1679 possibly at Nipisiguit, Acadie. They had 4 girls. All names not listed. #1, b.c. 1680; #2, b.c. 1682; #3, b.c. 1684; #4, b.c. 1688, all at Nipisiguit, Acadie. Listed age 35 on 1686 Nepisigny, Port Royal Census and wife as Indian. They had 3 servants with land and cattle.
Source – DGDFA & MNH & CENSUS 1686 & LRAMD

ESQUIMAUX
Marie-Catherine Esquimaux, appartenant a M. Desauniers, born 1723, baptized 19 May 1739 at Quebec. No marriage listed. Source – TD

FAFARD - QUEROTI (HURON)
Jean-Baptiste Fafard, son of Jean married 4 Nov. 1715 at Detroit to Marguerite Queroti, daughter of Joseph, (Huron Indians). Children were: Marguerite, baptism 1722, died 19 April 1728; Marie-Anne, baptism 30 Aug. 1724; Nicolas, baptism 27 July 1727.

Jean is the son of Marguerite Couc and Jean Fafard and grandson of Pierre Couc and Marie Mite8ameg8k8e.

Refer to
http://www.leveillee.net/ancestry/d294.htm#marguerite
There are several files (PRDH) on the site with information
about Fafard:
http://www.leveillee.net/ancestry/individu50.htm
http://www.leveillee.net/ancestry/famille13691.htm
Both of these list his wife's name as Marguerite DAGNES
married on 4 Nov 1715 in Ste-Anne-de-Détroit.
Under the parent's PRDH file
http://www.leveillee.net/ancestry/union5626.htm
Jean Baptiste is listed as the oldest of three children.
Source – TD & LEV & PRDH

FLEET – METIS
William Fleet born about 1783 married Widow, Metis who
was born 1775 in the North West Territories (West of the
Mississippi). Source – MNH

FONTENAY – SAUTEUSE
Francois Fontenay married Marie de Sauteuse (Indian)
(Source on page 687). Source – TD

GAGNE – (INDIEN - BERNARD)
Louis (indien-Bernard), son of Jocobis (Indien-Bernard) and
Suzanne Vincent married Marie-Etudienne Gagne 22 Jan.
1878 at Becancour, Quebec. Source – MBQ
GAGNON – KAORATE
Jean-Baptiste Gagnon married Cecile de Kaorate (Indian)
(Source on page 688). Source – TD

GAGNON – QUATREPATTE
Joseph Gagnon, Sauvage (Indian) married Angelique
Quatrepatte, a Sauvagesse (Indian). Date not given, but listed
on page 532 of source. Child was, Nicolas, baptism 18 Aug.
1758 at Trois-Pistoles, Quebec. (Source TD listed on page
688). Source – DNCF & TD

GAGNON – SAUVAGESSE
Pierre Gagnon, Le Sauvage (Indian), baptism 1709, died 31 Aug. 1773 at Kamouraska, Quebec, married Marie-Anne, a Sauvagesse (Indian). Date not given, but listed on page 534 of source. Children were: Pierre, baptism 12 April 1732 at Rimouski, Quebec; Marie, baptism 1740, died 6 Jan. 1741; Marie-Madeleine, baptism 5 Feb. 1748; Germain, baptism 11 June 1750; Marie-Olive, baptism 3 Aug. 1754 at l'Islet, Quebec; Louis, baptism 7 May 1758. Source – DNCF & TD

GAKERIENNENTA (INDIAN?) - NORMAND
Therese Gakeriennenta (possible Indian) married 12 Feb. 1760 to Charles Normand at Lac-des-Deux-Montagnes.
Source – TD

GARAND (SAUVAGE) - ?
Joseph Garand, a savage married Anne ......? around Nov. 1669. Children were: Catherine, born 14 June 1685 at Sorel, Quebec. Source – TD

GAUDIN – AGNES-TAMMEQUET
Nicolas Gaudin married Marie Agnes-Tammequet, a Sauvagesse (Indian). (or wife #1 Agnes, #2 Marie, Sauvagesse) Date not given but listed on page 548 of source. Children were: Pierre, baptism 24 Feb. 1749 at Rimouski, Quebec; Antoine, baptism 1 Nov. 1750; Reine, baptism 27 Aug. 1752; Louis, baptism 21 Sept. 1755; Madeleine, baptism 26 March 1758. Source – DNCF & TD

GAUTHIER-ST-GERMAIN-DE-VERVILLE – AMIOT (METIS)
Claude Gauthier-St-Germain-de-VerVille married 2 Oct. 1736 in Mackinac to Marie Louise Villeneuve Amiot, daughter of Daniel-Joseph Amiot and Louise. She was born 10 Jan. 1719/20 in Michilimackinac, Mackinac County, Michigan. She died 1757. Source – BKR

GAUTHIER – LAFRAMBOISE

Germain Gauthier dit St. Germain, Normandie, France was born 1643 and came to New France (Quebec) in 1665. His son, Pierre was born in 1684 and he died in 1761. He married Marie Ann Tessler and had a son, Pierre Paul Gauthier who married in 1770 to a Pawnee woman named Charlotte Laframboise. They had a son named Antoine Pierre Gauthier who married Elizabeth Aubertin. They had a son named Joseph Toussaint Gauthier, born 1821 and died 1913. His wife was Aurelie DesRoches. They had a daughter Aurelia Guathier, born 1874, died 1938. She married Louis Brazeau of Roxton Falls. Their son, Emile Brazeau was born in Strasbourg in 1890. (This line is still under question regarding the Pawnee bloodline). Source – Metis

GAUTIER (SAGUINGOIRA) – CAPE18SUEC8E

Jean Gautier (Saguingoira) Sr., baptism 28 Sept. 1669 son of Pierre Gautier and Charlotte Roussel married Marie Suzanne Cape18suec8e (Capciouekoue) Indian 1701. Children were: Marie, baptism 6 Jan. 1702 at Kaskakia; Domitilde, baptism, 14 Nov. 1703; Jean, baptism 19 Jan. 1707; Jean baptism, 11 Jan. 1713, Kaskaskia, Illinois who married Panis Sioux and had a daughter Catherine Gauthier (Metis), born 1755 who married Jean Baptiste Brunet. Source – DNCF & DGA & TD

GILL (INDIEN) – ST. AUBIN

Amable Gill (Indien), daughter of John-Baptiste Gill (indien) and Marguerite Poichar married Louis St. Aubin (Indien), son of Noel St-Aubin and Marie-Josette Rotoneau 30 Sept. 1850 at Becancour, Quebec. Source – MBQ

GILL – ABENAQUISE

Joseph-Louis Gill, son of Samuel Gill and Rosalie James married #1 Marie Jeanne Abenaquise. (Died before 1763) Date of marriage not given but listed on page 577 of source. #2 Marie-Julienne-Suz Gamelin, baptism 1742 daughter of Antoine. Source – DNCF & TD

GILL – JAMES
Samuel Gill of Nouvelle-Angleterre Amene par les Abenokis (Possible Indian) married Rosalie James of same place (Possible Indian). Date not given but listed on page 577 of source. Source – DNCF

GODFROY – TAOUES
Rene Godfroy-DeNormanville, De Linctot, son of Michel Godfroy and Perine Picote married Therese Taoues (Sauvagesse Indian). Date not given but listed on page 593 of source. Child was Charles-Marie, baptism 15 Feb. 1717 at Montreal, Quebec. Source – DNCF & TD

GODIN
Marie-Renee, baptized 24 June 1776 at la Baie-St-Paul, Quebec, daughter of Jacques-Rene and Madeleine Godin. Marie-Renee listed under Sauvages. Source – TD

GOGUET – PANIS-TIGNANCOUR
Francois Goguet (Sansoucy) married Marie Madaleine Panis-Tignancour, daughter of Damour (Indian origin). No date given but listed on page 594 of source. Source – DNCF & TD

GORY – PANIE
Jean Gory married Isabeau Panie (Indian), daughter of Jacques Panie and Marie Pousset of St-Maclou, Rouen, (France). Source – TD

GOUIN – OUILINCOTIA
Joseph-Nicolas Gouin, son of Claude Gouin and M. Josephte Cuilierier married c. 1775 to Mie (de 8ilincotia) Ouilincotia (Miamis Indian), died possibly before 1781. Date not given but listed on page 600 of source. Son was Charles, born June 1776, baptism 30 Dec. 1778 at Detroit. Joseph's #2 married was 1 Sept. 1781 to Archange Boyer, baptism 1759, daughter of Ignace. Their children was Pierre, baptism 31 Oct. 1781; Colette, baptism 19 Sept. 1782. Source – DNCF & TD

GOULET – BEAUCHAMP

Charles Goulet, son of Charles Goulet and Marie Francoise Illinoise (Indian) married M. Madeleine Beauchamp, daughter of Jean Beauchamp and Jeanne Muloin 24 May 1751 at Lachenaye, Quebec. Source – DNCF & TD

GOULET – ILLINOISE

Charles Goulet, baptism 1698, died 5 June 1748 at Lachenaye, son of Thomas Goulet and Marie Pancatelin married Marie Francoise Illinoise (Indian) 1719. Son was Charles, baptism 1719, married 24 May 1751 to Marie-Madeleine Beauchamp who died 21 April 1774. Source – DNCF & TD

GOULET – METIS

The Honorable Roger Goulet was born in 1834 and was the godson and protégé of Msgr. Provencher was listed a French Metis who became a surveyor, a district judge and a member of the Assiniboin Council. His parents are not listed. Source – OFCA – XI

GUEDRY – KESK8A (AMERINDIENNE)

Claude Guedry dit Grivois dit Laverdure, b.c. 1648 is listed with an Amerindienne girl with surname of Kesk8A in 1681. He is married to her in 1680 (2nd. wfie) possibly at St. John at Menagoeck/Mirligueche, Acadie. Children were: Jeanne, baptized 2 June 1681. Witnesses/sponsors were Claude Petitpas and Jeanne de la tour, wife of Martin. Source – DGDFA & LRAMD

GUILLEMOT - OUABENAQUIQUOY

Jean Guillemot, baptism 1694, son Jacques-Francois married #1 before 1733 to Catherine Ouabenaquiquoy, #2, 20 Feb. 1734 at Montreal, Quebec to Charlotte Marchand, baptism 1709 daughter of Nicolas. Source – TD

GUILLORY & BLONDEAU – AMIOT (METIS)
Ann Villeneuve4 Amiot, born 8 March 1714/15, died 8 Nov.
1757 was the daughter of Daniel-Joseph Amiot and Louise
Nepveuouikabe (Indian). She married first to Antoine
Guillory, second to B. Blondeau. Source – BKR

GUISHE (SAUVAGES)
Jean-Isidore (Guishe) Sauvages, a Micmac, baptism 30 Nov.
1715 at Quebec. No marriage listed. Source – TD

GRAND-CLAUDE (AMERINDIEN)
Rene Grand-Claude, b.c. 1685, son of Grand-Claude and
Marie Medosset (Both Amerindienne) married #1 Marie ?, b.c.
1691. Children were: Cecile, b.c. 1707. Rene married #2
Francoise Mius, b.c. 1697, daughter of Philippe Mius and
Marie. No children listed for them. Source – DGDFA

GRAND-CLAUDE (AMERINDIEN) – MEDOSSET
(AMERINDIENNE)
Grand-Claude, an Amerindien, b.c. 1640 married 1685 to
Marie Medosset (Medechese), an Amerindienne, b.c. 1653.
Children were: Rene, b.c. 1685, married #1 Marie ? and #2 in
1725 to Francoise Mius, daughter of Philippe and Marie;
Claude, b.c. 1687 married Marie Pierre; Marie-Catherine, b.c.
1689; Joseph, b.c. 1691; Martin, b.c. 1693 married Marguerite
Joseph, daughter of Francois Joseph and Marie Egighighe;
Francois, b.c. 1698. Source – DGDFA

HACHE (LARCHE) – (AMERINDIENNE)
Pierre Hache (Larche) dit Gallant was born c. 1662 at Tri-
Riviere, Quebec. He married an Amerindienne in Acadie.
They had a son, Michel, born 1668 who married 1690 to Anne
Cormier, born 1674 daughter of Thomas Cormier and Marie
Madeleine Girouard. Their children were all listed as (dit
Gallant): Michel, b. c. 1691, married Madeleine LeBlanc;
Joseph, b.c. 1693, married Marie Gaudet; Marie, b.c. 1694,

married Francois Poirier, and Rene Rassicot; Jean-Baptiste b.c. 1696, married Anne-Marie (Marie-Anne) Gentil; Charles, b.c. 1698, married Genevieve Lavergne; Pierre, b.c. 1701, married Cecile Lavergne; Anne, b.c. 1703, married Joseph Pretieux; Marguerite, b.c. 1705, married Pierre Jacquemin; Francois, b.c. 1707, married Anne Boudrot; Marie-Madeleine, b.c. 1710, married Pierre Duval; Jacques, b.c. 1712, married Marie-Josephe Boudrot; Louise, b.c. 1716, married Louis Belliveau.

There is a PRDH file at http://www.leveillee.net/ancestry/union10983.htm to which was added the data from Stephen White.
Source – DGDFA & LEV & PRDH

HAMELIN – SAUTEUSE
Charles Hamelin (Lagueniere La Guenier), son of Jacques Hamelin and Antoinette Richard, (Voyageur) married Marie-Anas (Atha) Athanase (Indian) de Sauteuse 27 Nov. 1738 at Michillimackinac. And married again to M. Anastasia Sauteuse (Indian) 4 Feb. 1748 at same place.
Source – DNCF & TD

HAMELIN - SAUVAGEAU
Joseph-Marie Hamelin, son Joseph-Marie married 25 Feb. 1783 at Deschambault to Marie-Louise Sauvageau (Possible Indian?), baptism 1755, daughter of Joseph. Child was Marie-Joseph, baptism 1 Dec. 1783 at Grondines. Source – TD

HAMELIN – LE SABLE
Luis Hamelin, son of Charles Hamelin and M. Athanase Sauteuse (Indian) married M. Josephte Le Sable (Indian). Date not given but listed on page 644 of source. Source – DNCF

HERY (DUPLANTY) – MISSALIN8D8E

Louis Hery (Duplanty), baptism 26 July 1711, son of Jacques Hery and Jeanne Vanier married 1749 to Marie-Anastasie Missalin8d8e of the Sauteux Nation 1749. Children were: Marie-Charlotte, baptism 9 Nov. 1750 at Lac-des-Deux-Montagnes; Marie-Madeliene, baptism 4 Dec. 1752; Louis, baptism 24 Dec. 1754; Marie-Angelique, baptism 25 June 1758; Elisabeth, baptism 23 June 1760; Marie-Catherine, baptism 23 April 1765, died 28 July 1765; Marie-Amable, baptism 14 July 1766. Source – DNCF & TD

HOGUE - NACHITA

Pierre Hogue of St. Malo, born 1648 married 27 Nov. 1673 to Catherine Nachita of the Puteotamite Nation, born 1654 and died 28 Sept. 1676 at Montreal, Quebec. One son, Claude Hogue was born 24 Oct. 1673. Tanguay says Pierre's parents were Jean Hogue and Nicole Dubus of N.D. of Bellefontaine, eveche d'Amiens. Children were: Claude, b. 24 Oct. 1673; Pierre, b. 9 July 1675 and died 23 April 1697 at Pointe-aux-Trembles in Montreal, Quebec. Pierre married #2 10 Nov. 1676 at Montreal, Quebec to Jeanne Theodore who was born 1663, the daughter of Michel Theodore. They had 6 children. Source – MC & TD

HOTESSE - LAHRENOUATHA

Zacharie Hotesse, second chief of the Huron's at Lorette married Charlotte Lahrenouatha (Possible Indian?). Child was Paul (Huron) who married 12 Jan. 1796 to Marie-Louise Galarneau, daughter of Louis at Quebec. Source – TD

HUIT

Infant Huit, an Algonquins born between June and Sept. 1695 at Montreal, Quebec. No marriage listed. Source – TD

HUQUERRE (LA REJOUISSANCE) – KOESKI
Francois Huquerre, son of Jean Huquerre and Marie Roux of
St. Sulpice d'Orleans, Orleanais, Peintre, France married M.
Madeleine Koeski of the Koeski Arabouska Sokokouis Nation
27 Nov. 1679 at Trois Rivieres, Quebec. Source – DNCF

HURONNE - MONTOUR
Elisabeth Huronne (Possible Huron Indian) married Joseph
Montour. Source – TD

HYARD - MICHAUD
Jean Hyard, "The Mongrel" was known as a Metis Indian, son
of Francois Hyard who married Marie-Charlotte Michaud,
daughter of Pierre Michaud and Madeliene Cadieu married 23
July 1769 at Kamouraska, Quebec. Children were: Guilli, b.c.
25 July 1761 and Jean Hyard, born 12 Oct. 1763.
Source – GFH

JACOB – ORUATAYON
Jean-Baptiste Jacob, baptism 1731 son of Jean-Baptiste Jacob
and Marie Serrow of Londres, Angleterre, France. Married #1
to Francoise Oruatayon (Sauvagesse) 30 Jan. 1753 at St-Anne-
de-la-Perade. Her baptism was 1715, died 27 Dec. 1755.
Children were, Jean-Baptism 8 Oct. 1753; Marie, died 9 Dec.
1755. Number 2 marriage was 20 Nov. 1757 to Marie-Joseph
Gervais, batism 1740, daughter of Louis-Joseph. They had 14
children, another with same name as first child (Jean-Baptiste)
with Francoise Oruatayon. Source – DNCF & TD

JACQUES – (DENYS)
Pierre Jacques married Marie-Anne Denys (Indian line),
daughter of Noel Denys and Helen Millier 9 Nov. 1852 at
Becancour, Quebec. Source – MBQ

JACQUES - ABENAQUISE
Pierre Jacques married Marie-Anne Abenaquise after 1700.
Source – TD

JACQUES - ABENAQUISE
Pierre Jacques married Marie-Anne Abenaquise (Possible
Indian). Child was Francois-Xavier, baptism 6 Feb. 1743 at
St-Antoine-Tilly. Source – TD

JANOT – MINAOURE
Mr. Janot married M. Anne Minaoure of the Micmac Nation.
No date given but listed on page 690 of source.
Source – DNCF & TD

JOLIVET – PACHAT
Charles-Francois Jolivet of Aime et Anne Fiset married
Marguerite Pachat of the Panise Nation 4 April 1731 at
Montreal, Quebec. Source – DNCF

JOSEPH (AMERINDIEN)
Francois Joseph dit Lejeune is listed as an Amerindien born
around 1648 married 1673 to Jeanne Lejeune dit Briard who
was born around 1651. She married again in 1694 to Jean
Gaudet. The children by Francois were: Edmee (Aimee), b.c.
1674 who married Charles Chauvet dit La Gerne; Jean, b.c.
1675; Cecile, b.c. 1680 married 1694 to Etienne Rivet and
again in 1708 to Martin Corporon; Francois, b.c. 1682 married
Marie Egighighe; Anne, b.c. 1684; Catherine, b.c. 1685
married 7 Jan. 1720 to Jean Comeau. The children adopted the
mother's surname (Lejeune) as many cases did when the
father was Indian. Source – DGDFA & DGDFA Eng Sup

JOSEPH – EGIGHIGHE
Francois Joseph dit Lejeune, son of Francois Joseph and
Jeanne LeJeune, born around 1682 married Marie Egighighe,
and Amerindienne. They had a daughter, Marguerite, b.c.
1710 who married 25 Feb. 1727 to Martin Grand-Claude, son
of Grand-Claude and Marie Medosset. Source – DGDFA

K8ASK8RI
Marie-Josette K8ask8ri, temiskaming, veuve d'un Algonquin,
born 19 et died 28 Dec. 1698 agees de 30 ans. Source – TD

KA8GORA
Charles Ka8gora, b. 6 Aug. 1684 at Chateau-Richer, Quebec.
Source – TD

KAPACHTCHE8NET
Marie-Anne, Tete-de-Boute of Chicoutimi, daughter of
Guillaume Kapachtche8net, born 1776, baptized 24 Dec. 1778
at Ste-Anne-de-la-Perade, Quebec. No marriage listed.
Source – TD

KARONYARAS
Pierre (Karonyaras), an Iroquois of Luc, baptized 27 March
1744 at Sault-au-Recollet, Quebec. No parents listed.
Source – TD

KELLER (CALER) – SKA8ENNATI
Daniel Keller (Caler), Alias Sonha8entas Claude of Angliais
Nation married Madaleine Ska8ennati. Date not given but
listed on page 714 of source. Death was 6 June 1761 at Lac
des Deux-Montagnes. Child was, Pierre, baptism 26 Nov.
1760, died 16 April 1761. Source – DNCF & TD

KESKABOG8ET
Marie-Etiennette Keskabog8et born 21 Sept. 1690 age 5 at
Riviere-Ouelle, Quebec. Source – TD

KICKACHIA

Marie-Louise (Kickachia), appartenant a M. Aubert, born 1709, baptized 16 May 1739 at Quebec. No marriage listed. Source – TD

KIONHATONI

Joseph-Nicolas (Kionhatoni) born at Mars and baptized 14 Sept. 1750 at Montreal, Quebec. (Son of Kionhatoni, orateur sauvage du nouvel establishment at la Presentation-de-la-Riviere-Hoegatsi, et de Onhatsouaten, dame du conseil du dit establishment.) Source – TD

KNIGHT – KINII8ENA

Amable Knight, husband of Catherine Kinii8ena. Source – TD

KNIGHT – SAUVAGESSE

Bath. Knight, husband of Marie Sauvagesse. Source – TD

KINGHT – SAUVAGESSE

Luc Knight, husband of Marie Sauvagesse. Source – TD

L'EVEILLE

Louis dit L'Eveille, appartenant a Francois Leveille, captain of navire, baptized 4 May 1747 at Quebec. (Les parents etaient de l'ancienne France et inconnus; il avait ete eleve par les Montagnais). No marriage listed.
Refer to http://www.leveillee.net/ancestry/individu50812.htm
http://www.leveillee.net/ancestry/familly84387.htm
and there are links to the PRDH database for members of this family, and grandchildren.
Source – TD & LEV & PRDH

L'EVEILLE – SAUVAGESSE

Barnabe L'Eveille married Marguerite Sauvagesse (Indian). Date and location not given, but located on page 855 of source. Children were: Louis, b. 1688, d. 19 Jan. 1689 at Cape Sante, Quebec; Claude, b. 1686, d. 25 March 1689. Source – DNCF & TD

LABAUVE (LABOVE) – LEJEUNE (KAGIGCONIAC)

Anne Lejeune dit Baiard, daughter of Martin Lejeune and Jeanne Kagigconiac (Amerindienne) married around 1702 to Rene Labauve dit Renochon who was born around 1679 possibly at Les Mines, Acadie. His parents were, Louis-Noel Labauve and Marie Rimbault who married at Les Mines, Acadie in 1678. Rene and Anne's children were: Pierre, b.c. 1703 possibly at La Heve, Acadie; Marie (-Josephe), b.c. 1706 at possibly La Heve, Acadie and married 1728 to Francois LeBlanc, son of Andre LeBlanc and Marie Dugas; Therese; Anne, b.c. May 1711 and married 18 Oct. 1728 to Jean Bourey, son of Andre Bourey and Catherine Cornu, and married again 14 April 1738 to Joseph Tudal, son of Yves Tudal and Jeanne Faumouchet. Source – DGDFA

LACHEVRATIERE – INDIAN

Joseph Lachevratiere married an Indian woman around 1800 possibly around Alberta, Canada. They had a daughter Marie Lachevretiere married 1825 to Joseph Vandal who was born 10 July 1798 at Sorel, Richelieu, Quebec. He was listed as the original white man from Sorel Quebec. He married again to Adelaide Charbonneau, daughter of Jean Baptiste Charbonneau and Louise Boucher on 8 Oct. 1850. (From the Charles D. Denny Papers Archives, Calgary, Alberta). Source – GMMF

LAFLEUR/COUP/COUC, MARIE ANGELIQUE

Listed in Trois-Rivieres, Quebec on 24 Oct. 1679 with sister Jeanne Couc, father, Pierre Couc Lafleur and mother Marie Miteouamegoukoue, a Algonquine. Born before 1662. Died 7 Jan. 1750 at Pointe-du-Lac, Quebec. Maried 30 Aug. 1682 at Sorel, Quebec to Francois Delpe St-Cerny, Lieutenant. Extensive and verified data on this family at http://www.leveillee.net/ancestry/d294.htm where research results from Norm Leveille and or Suzanne Boivin Sommerville's work has been compiled. Tanquay and Jette had many errors so the above site is worth checking out.
Source – JR & LEV

LAFLEUR/COUC, ISABELLE ELISABETH MARIE

Daughter of Pierre Couc (Lafleur) and Marie Miteouamegoukoue (Amerindienne) who married Joachim Germano/Germanau, Lieutenant, son of Joachim Germano and Marie Choufy of St-Maxime, Eveche (France?) on 30 April 1684 at Sorel, Quebec. She died in the English Colonies in 1752. Extensive and verified data on this family at http://www.leveillee.net/ancestry/d294.htm where research results from Norm Léveillée and or Suzanne Boivin Sommerville's work has been compiled. Tanquay and Jette had many errors so the above site is worth checking out.
Source – TD & LEV

LAFLEUR/COUC, JEAN

Born before 1673 to Pierre Couc Lafleur and Marie Miteouamegoukoue (Algonquine) and married before 24 Nov. 1706 to Anne. He was listed as a Lieutenant.
Extensive and verified data on this family at http://www.leveillee.net/ancestry/d294.htm where research results from Norm Léveillée and or Suzanne Boivin Sommerville's work has been compiled. Tanquay and Jette had many errors so the above site is worth checking out.
Source – JT & LEV

LAFLEUR/COUC, JEANNE

Was listed as age 20 on 24 Oct. 1679 at Trois-Rivieres, Quebec. She was the daughter of Pierre Couc Lafleur and Marie Miteouamegoukoue, an Algonquine. She is also listed in Baptism records at Trois-Riviere, Quebec (Mother listed as Indienne). And again in marriage record at St-Francois-du-Lac, Quebec on 7 Jan. 1688, age 32 marrying Louis Couc Montour of St-Francois. Jeanne is also listed as from St-Francois as her parents. Her name is recorded as Jeanne Quigetigoucoue (Algonquine). Born 14 July 1657 at Trois-Rivieres, Quebec. Died 23 Oct. 1679 at Trois-Rivieres, Quebec. Extensive and verified data on this family at http://www.leveillee.net/ancestry/d294.htm where research results from Norm Léveillée and or Suzanne Boivin Sommerville's work has been compiled. Tanquay and Jette had many errors so the above site is worth checking out.
Source – JR & LEV

LAFLEUR/COUC, MARIE MADELEINE

Born before 1669 to Pierre Couc Lafleur and Marie Miteouamegoukoue (Algonquine). She married Lieutenant Maurice Menard Fontaine.
Extensive and verified data on this family at http://www.leveillee.net/ancestry/d294.htm where research results from Norm Léveillée and or Suzanne Boivin Sommerville's work has been compiled. Tanquay and Jette had many errors so the above site is worth checking out.
Source – JR & LEV

LAFLEUR/COUC – MITEOUAMEGOUKOUE, MARIE

Algonquine who married Pierre Couc Lafleur, son of Nicolas Couc and Elisabeth Templair on 16 April 1657 at Trois-Rivieres, Quebec.
Extensive and verified data on this family at http://www.leveillee.net/ancestry/d294.htm where research results from Norm Léveillée and or Suzanne Boivin

Sommerville's work has been compiled. Tanquay and Jette had many errors so the above site is worth checking out. Norn Léveillée has extensive and all verified data on his 8th great-grandmother, Marie Mite8ameg8k8e (Proper Algonquin spelling).

Please refer to http://www.leveillee.net/ancestry/d296.htm . You'll find on this page reference to René Jetté's error at assigning the two witnesses at Pierre & Mite8ameg8k8e (Indians had only one name) as her mother and father, translating "Carolus" latin for Charles as "Carole." This error has been propagated throughout the genealogy references. Norm tries to send an email to people who still have this error on their web pages.

He wrote a "romantic" story about my 8th great-grandmother at http://www.leveillee.net/ancestry/mariem.htm

Source – JR & LEV

LAFLEUR/COUC - MARGUERITE

She was the daughter of Pierre Couc Lafleur and Marie Miteouamegoukoue who was baptized on 5 June 1664 at Trois-Rivieres, Quebec. Mother, Marie was listed as an Amerindienne. She married Jean Fafard.

Extensive and verified data on this family at http://www.leveillee.net/ancestry/d294.htm where research results from Norm Léveillée and or Suzanne Boivin Sommerville's work has been compiled. Tanquay and Jette had many errors so the above site is worth checking out.

Source – JR & LEV

LAFORCE - GA8ENNONTIE

Ignace Laforce married Marie Ga8ennontie before 1765. Child was, Therese, baptism 30 Sept. at Lac-des-Deux-Montagnes.

Source – TD

LAFOND/LANFOND - ANANONTHA

Jean de Lanfond (Indian?), born 1640, son of Etienne, died 10 May 1716 at Batiscan married first to Catherine Senecal, daughter of Adrien. Married record of son Jean-Baptiste says he was part Indian. Children were: Marie, b. 1671 who married 3 Feb. 1687 at Amable Breillard; Jean, b. 1675 who married Marie Richaume; Catherine, b. 1677 who married 23 Nov. 1694 to Francois Cosset; Etienne, b. 1679 who married 3 Feb. 1707 to Jeanne Louineau at Quebec; Marguerite, b. 8 Nov. 1682, died 23 May 1685; Marguerite, b. 26 July 1685, married #1 25 July 1703 to Joseph Fafard, #2 13 Jan. 1710 to Jean-Baptiste Courchene; Pierre, b. 25 April 1688 who married 13 August 1715 to Jeanne Lefebvre; Marie-Renee, b. 11 March 1692 who married 17 Feb. 1716 to Damien Tifaut. Pierre Lanfond married #2, 28 August 1697 at Batiscan to Catherine Ananontha (Indian), baptism 1649 previous wife of Jacques Couturier. Source – TD

LAGRAVE – OUABANQIS

Pierre Lagrave married Francoise Ouabanois (Indian) on 1673 in Quebec. Tanguay says, Children were: Pierre, b. 1674, died 11 July 1703 at Montreal, Quebec; Charles, baptism 1692, died 22 Nov. 1727, married 8 Jan. 1720 to Marie-Anne Guibord at St. Anne de la Perade, Quebec.
Source – DNCF & TD

LEJEUNE - MICMAC

Pierre Lejeune, born c. 1595, Martiaize, Loudon, France, died after 1636, Port Royal, Acadie. He immigrated to Port Royal, Acadia c. 1611 with Poutrincourt and Biencourt. Married a MicMac girl c. 1622. Her name is unknown at this time but they had the following children; Edmee, b.c. 1624, Martiaize, France, married Francois Gauterot 1644, Martaiza, France (Did this family go back to France or is there another mother to Edmee?). She died 1687, Port Royal, Acadie; Pierre, b. c. 1625, Acadie, Canada or Brie, France?, married Marguerite(?)

Doucet (Possible Micmac descent), c. 1650 at Port Royal, Acadie, died after 1704; Catherine, b. 1633, Port Royal, Acadie, Canada, married Francois Savoie c. 1652, Port Royal, Acadie. She died after 1671, Port Royal.

LAMBERT – MICMAC

Jehan/Jean Antoine Lambert, b. c. 1591, Strong Lomeron. Acadie, Canada, married c. 1621 to Radgonde (Micmac/Mi'Kmaq) Indian who was born at Acadie. Daughter was Jeanne Radegonde Lambert, b. 1621, Strong Lomeron, Cape de Sable, Acadie, Canada. Jean and Rodgonde went to France and came back. Oral Micmac history claims she was a Micmac/Mi'kmaq Indian. So far no written proof, but strong oral history.

There is a controversy about Jeanne Radegonde Lambert. Stephen White has made no mention of her Mi'kmaq origins. And yet, there is historical and oral tradition indicating that she was Mi'kmaq. White based himself solely on written documents, as most of the genealogists do today. Many of his resources were written by the Catholic clergy, who at a certain period in time, wanted to erase any reference to the "pagan" Native Americans. However, historical and oral tradition among the Native Americans and/or the Metis do have value in research.

Refer to http://www.leveillee.net/ancestry/d739.htm
But also, take a look at the genealogy section of http://www.metisduquebec.ca/
Source – MISC & LEV

LAMBERT – TAMESSE

Marie-Agathe Lambert married Guillaume Tamesse (Indian), son of Pierre Tamesse and Francoise Rousseau 8 Jan. 1776 at Becancour, Quebec. Source – MBQ

LAMOUREUX - PIGAROUICHE (SAVAGE)
Pierre Lamoureux, son of Jean married #1 Marguerite
Pigarouiche, Sauvagesse (Savage) who was born 1647.
Children were Marie-Renee, b. 1672 who married 22 Sept.
1693 to Jacques Hery at Montreal, Quebec; Jacques, b. 1673.
Pierre married #2 Barbe Celles, daughter of Gabriel 2 Oct.
1684 at Montreal, Quebec. Source – TD

LAMOUREAX – PIGAROUICHE
Pierre Lamoureax (St-Germain), baptism 1649, died 30 Dec.
1740 at Bout-de-i'lle, M, Quebec, son of Jean Lamoureax and
M. Madeleine De Vienne married Marguerite Pigarouiche, a
Sauvagesse (Indian), baptism 1647 in 1670. Child was,
Francois, baptism 1675, married Marguerite Menard.
Source – DNCF & TD

LANGLADE (LANGLOIS?) – METIS
Charles Langlade, a mixed-blood Metis led 250 Ojibwe and
Ottawa warriors from Mackinac in an attack on the British
trading post and Miami village at Pickawillany (Piqua, Ohio)
dated June 1752. Source – HH

LANGLOIS - MAIAWADJIWAIWKWE
Julie Maiawadjiwakwe (Indian). She married, Mr. Langlois.
Child was William Bomakeghick/Bamejijik who married
Anchangele Otishkwagamin LeClaire. Source – BKR

LANGLOIS – SAUVAGESSE
Joseph-Marie Langlois, baptism 22 April 1739, son of Jean-
Francois Langlois and Therese Bertrand married Lisette
Sauvagesse (Indian) married 28 Oct. 1782 at St-Louis,
Missouri. Source – DNCF & TD

LANGLOIS – ALGONQUINE

Pierre Langlois married Madeleine Algonquine. There is no date or location but listed on page 757 of source. Tanguay has one child, Louis, baptism 5 June 1742 at Trois-Rivieres, Quebec. Source – DNCF & TD

LAROCQUE, MARGUERITE (METIS)

Was born between 1800 and 1805. Died possible before 1847. She married Emanuel Beaugrand dit Champagne before 1820. Their children were: Emanuel Champagne Jr., born c. 1820; Marguerite, born June 1827; Jostette (Josephte), born 12 June 1828 at St. Boniface, MB; Jean Baptiste, born between 1828-1832; Pierre, born 14 May 1833 at St. Boniface, MB; Marie, born 1839; Lucie, born 1841; Maxime, born 14 Aug. 1845. Emanuel Sr. marries again in 1847 to Madeleine Laderoute at St. Boniface and had children: David, born 24 Sept. 1848; Caoline, born 24 Dec. 1850; Esther, born 22 Dec. 1855. Source – CAF

LASNIER – AMERINDIENNE

Louis Lasnier, born in Dieppe, Picardie, France had a son by a Canadienne (Amerindienne). The record is dated 1619, but unmarried is referenced. This son was Andre Lasnier who was born around 1620, first Acadian born. Location was Port Latour, Cape Sable, Acadie. His mother is recorded as a Mi'Kmaq. Andre was rebaptized in France 27 Dec. 1632. Source – DGDFA & MA

LATOUR (LA TOUR) – SAUVANGESSE)

Latour (La Tour), b. 1624, d. 16 Feb. 1704, Judge of Champlain married Louise Sauvangesse (Indian). Location, names and dates not listed, but located on page 772 of source. Source – DNCF & TD

LATOUR – (ACADIE NATIVE NORTH AMERICAN)

Charles LaTour, de Saint Etienne, born c. 1596, Saint Etienne, France, son of Claude Turgis LaTour and Marie Amador de Salazar, from Champagne, France He died 1663 at age 67 and his ashes rest within Acadie. He married first to an Acadie Mi'kmaq Native North American c. 1623 at Port La Tour, Acadie. Her name has not been found nor her parents yet. She was born c. 1600 in Acadie and died between 1627-32 in Acadie. They had three children; A Female born after 1623, a female, Jeanne La Tour born 1626, another female, Antoinette La Tour, born 1627 who became the first Benedictine nun in North America in 1642. The Queen of France tried to keep her in France to sing for her along with others, but she refused and went back to Canada. Source – LRA

LATOUR - D'APRENDESTIGUY

Jeanne Latour, daughter of Charles de St-Etienne de La Tour, his eldest daughter born about 1626. Her monther was an Ameridian of Cap Sable, Acadie. (Dictionnaire, p. 1433). Between 1655-56 Jeanne marries Martin d'Aprendestiguy de Martignon. They had one daughter, Marie-Anne d'Aprendestiguy married Guilliaume Bourgeois, son of Jacques. This line continues into the LeBlanc genealogy. Source – LRAMD

LEAN – KAHAWABIK

Michael Lean married Agnes Kahawabik (Indian). Their daughter Lexilia Lean married Nicolas Crate/Crete, son of Paul Crate/Crete and Elisabeth Allard 16 Feb. 1852 at Chapeau, Pontiac County, Quebec. The source from the Pontiac County, Quebec Catholic Church Marriages 1836-1973 records and listed on the Metis net page. Source – Metis

LE BASQUE – AMERINDIENNE

Pierre Le Basque of Bayonne married 1686 to an Amerindienne and had an enfant (no name listed) who was born around 1687 at Baie des Chaleurs, Acadie. Source – DGDFA

LEBUC – L'HERAULT

Louis Leduc was a native of the Chicachias nation and married Marie Madeleine L' Herault after 1701 in or near Montreal, Quebec. She was the youngest daughter of eight children to Sixte l'Herault and Reine Deblois who were married 15 Feb. 1694. Marie Madeleine first married Jean Laroche, son of Robert Laroche and Jeanne Souillou who were from France. They had 7 children before he died. Marie Madeleine died after her second husband Louis Leduc at Laprairie, Quebec in 1741. Louis is listed in Tanguay's book but it is not know if they had children together.
Source – OFCA – IX

LEGARDEUR – PANISE

Charles Legardeur married Suzanne Panise (Indian) (on page 688). Source – TD

LEJEUNE (AMERINDIENNE)

Claude Lejeune, b.c. 1686, son of Martin (Briard) (Labriere) Lejeune and Jeanne Kagigconiac (Amerindienne) of Port Maltais, Acadie married 14 Sept. 1705 at Port Royal, Acadie to Anne-Marie Gaudet, born 1689, daughter of Jean Gaudet and Jeanne Henry of Petite-Riviere. Children were: Marie-Josephe who married 19 Nov. 1725 to Martin Benoit, son of Pierre l'aine Benoit and Marie Forest; Marguerite born between 20 May and 7 July 1719 who married 1752 to Charles Roy, son of Jean Roy and Jeanne Lejeune. Source – DGDFA

LEJEUNE – JOSEPH

In this case it appears the male is the North American Native. Franois Joseph record says he was from Savage Nation. Steve White's book says that children of a Metis family usually took the mother's last name. He married Jeanne LeJeune. They had a daughter, Catherine Joseph, but could be LeJeune? She married Jean Comeau on 7 Jan. 1720 at Port Royal, Acadie. Not much more on this line. Source – OFCA-XXIV

LEJEUNE – KAGIGCONIAC

Martin Lejeune dit Briard (Lebriere), born around 1661 at La Heve, son of Pierre Lejeune and ….? Doucet (Daughter of Germain Doucet) married in 1684 to Jeanne Marie Kagigconiac, an Amerindienne. She died before 1699. He married again in 1699 to Marie Gaudet, daughter of Jean Gaudet and Jeanne Henry. And married again on 16 Oct. 1729 to Marie Arnault (Remaud) dit Grislard. The children of Martin and Jeanne Marie were: Claude (Briard), b.c. 1686, died 19 Nov. 1725, and married 14 Sept. 1705 to Anne-Marie Gaudet, daughter of Jean Gaudet and Jeanne Henry; A daughter, b.c. 1686; Anne (Briard), b.c. 1687 at La Heve, Acadie and married 1702 to Rene dit Renochon Labauve, son of Louis-Noel Labauve and Marie Rimbault; Germain, b.c. 1689 at Le Heve, Acadie; Bernard, b.c. 1693 at Le Heve, Acadie. Source – DGDFA & AMD

LEJEUNE – KAGIGCONIAC (Same Martin as above)

Martin (Briard/Labriere) Lejeune married 1684 at Acadie, Canada to Jeanne Marie Kagigconiac, an Amerindienne. Their children were: Claude (Briard) Lejeune, Anne (Briard) Lejeune, Germain Lejeune, Bernard Lejeune. Listed on 1686 Port Royal Census at age 25, and Jeanne was listed as an Indian. Children were, Claude and a female.
Source – MNH & CENSUS 1686

LEJEUNE – KAGIGCONIAC

Martin Lejeune, son of Martin was baptized in 1705 and his Godmother was Catherine Kagigconiac.
Source – DGDFA & MNH

LEJEUNE – KAGIGCONIAC

Paul Lejeune, son of Martin Godmother was Marguerite Kagigconiac 1705 in Acadie. Source – DGDFA

LEPELE - 8TA8OISE

Claude-Joseph LePele, baptism 13 Aug. 1724, died 10 Dec. 1757, son of Claude, son of Claude and Marie-Anne Lanfond, daughter of Pierre, married 10 May 1756 to Marie-Jeanne 8ta8oise (Mighissens) (Indian) at Michillimakinac. Child was Marie-Anne, born 10 March 1757, baptism 20 May 1757. Source – TD

LETELLIER - 8ET8KIS

Antoine Letellier, baptism 1733, son Jean-Baptiste married 16 July 1753 at Michillimakinac to Charlotte 8et8kis (Indian). Children were, Jean-Baptiste, born 10 Sept. 1754, baptiste 17 June 1755; Charles, born 20 Nov. 1757 at Fond-du-Lac, baptism 2 July 1758; Nicolas, baptism 24 June 1759; Joseph, baptism 30 May 1761; Ignace, born 5 Jan. 1763 at Haut-Wisconsin, baptism 30 June 1763; Antoine, born 23 Jan. 1765 at Mississippi, baptism 30 June 1765. Source – TD

LETELLIER – NIPISSING

Jean-Baptiste Letellier married Marie-Joseph de Nipissing (Indian) (on page 688). Source – TD

LETELLIER – MACATEMIC8C8E

Rene-Francois Letellier, baptism 1747, son of Jean-Baptiste Letellier and M. Josephte Nipissing married …, Macatemic8c8e (Indian). No date or location given, but listed on page 850 of source. Child was Francois, born 1 Jan. 1764, baptism 3 July 1765 at Michillimakinac. Source – DNCF & TD

LIENARD - SAUVAGESSE

Jean-Francois Lienard, b. 29 Aug. 1657, parents, Sebastien Lienard and Francoise Pelletier married #1 to Marie Madeleine Sauvagesse, #2 to Agnes Robitaille. He died 25 Feb. 1724 at Pointe-aux-Trembles at Quebec. Source – TD

LIENARD-DURBOIS - WABANQUIQUOIS
Joacqine Francois Lienard-Durbois, son of Sebastien, born 20
March 1671, died 25 Feb. 1724 at Pointe-aux-Trembles at
Quebec married #1 Marie-Madeleine Arpot Wabanquiquois.
They had a son, Francois. #2 married was on 16 Oct. 1713 to
Marie Agnes Cormeau. They had 3 children. Source – TD

LIMOGES/LIMOUSIN – TEGANIHA
Louis Limoges, son of Martin Limoges and Marie Renote of
Ste-Maure-de-Touraine, diocese of Tours, Touraine, France.
Louis was a soldier of M. De Varennes who married Marie
Teganiha, an Iroquoise. Not date or place given, but listed on
page 863 of source. Source – DNCF & TD

LORRAIN – NAGDOTIEOUE
Joseph Lorrain son of Pierre Lorrain and Francoise Saulnier
was the godson of Gilbert Barbier, baptisted 7 June 1677. He
was employed to travel with Jean Beaujean on 26 March 1692
to the Outaouais; then later to Michillimackinac and then to
the Illinois. Around 1700 he married Cunegonde Nagdotieoue,
an Illinois woman. They had only one daughter, Marie who
married Francois Allard at Kaskaskia on 20 Oct. 1726.
Francois was the son of Joseph Allard and Marthe Delugre
who married at Sainte-Anne du Petit-Cap Quebec on 9 Nov.
1690. Source – OFCA – XXI

LORRAIN – PANISE
…….. Lorrain married Catherine Panise (Indian) (on page
688). Source – TD

MACOUS - OUTAOUAISE
…… Macous married ……… Outaouaise (Indian). Child was
Marguerite, born 1752, baptism 19 Dec. 1762 at Detroit
(Michigan). Source – TD

MACOUS DIT FAFARD – ANGOUIROT/ANG8IROT
Joseph Macous, died 10 Oct. 1768 at Detroit (Michigan)
married Marie-Jeanne Angouirot (Huronne). Child was Marie-
Catherine, baptism 12 March 1758. Source – TD

MAILLOT (SAUVAGES)
Charles Maillot (Sauvages), born 1711, et Augustin Laprise,
born 1712, baptism 17 Oct. 1718 at Quebec. (Petits sauvages
Panis appartenant a M. Denis Roberge, capitaine de vaisseau).
Source – TD

MANA8IAT - LANGEVIN
Jean-Baptiste Mana8iat, sauvage (Indian) de Tadoussac
married 21 Jan. 1709 at St-Nicolas to Madeleine Langevin.
Source – TD

MAN8K8E
Marie-Madeleine Man8k8e, an Algonquine, born 1699, died
11 June 1699 at Montreal, Quebec. Source – TD

MARECHAL – ILLINOISE
Nicolas Marechal of St. Vincent, diocese of Verdun, Lorraine,
Verdum, Bourgogne, France married Mare-Jeanne, an Illinoise
(Indian) in 1744. Children were; Marie-Joseph, baptism 28
Sept. 1745 at Cahokia; Marie-Catherine, baptism 19 Oct.
1747, married 6 Sept. 1767 to Francois Moreau at St. Louis,
Missouri; Jean-Baptiste, baptism 29 Aug. 1749; Francois,
baptism 31 March 1751, married 1775 to Marie-Therese
Riviere; Marie-Suzanne, baptism 23 July 1753, died 20 Aug.
1754; Jacques, married 1784 to Genevieve Cardinal; Antoine,
baptism 1754, married 7 Jan. 1777 to Catherine Tabeau;
Joseph, baptism 13 Oct. 1755; Marie-Elisabeth, baptism 1
Nov. 1757, married #1 19 Jan. 1774 to Antoine Martin, #2 20
Feb. 1791 to Jean-Baptiste Primeau. Source – DNCF & TD

MARIE – LE GRAND

Jean Marie, son of Jacques Marie and Madeleine Hersan of Montchaton, diocese of Coutance, Normandie, France married Jeanne Le Grand, daughter of Louis Le Grand and Madeleine Sauvagesse (Indian) of I'lle of Terre-Neuve at Quebec on 30 Oct. 1747. Children were: Marie-Angelique, born 4 Oct. 1740; Marie-Catherine, born 26 Sept. 1742; Marie-Jeanne, born 2 Feb. 1745; Marie-Charlotte, born 18 Feb. 1747. Source – DNCF & TD

MARTIN – MICMAC

Etienne Martin, Sauvage (Indian) married Charlotte Micmac (Indian) 1735. Children were; Marie-Anne, baptism 1736, died 16 Feb. 1743 at Kamouraska; Marie-Anne, baptism 11 Feb. 1739, died 14 June 1740; Joseph-Marie, baptism 12 March 1741; Marie, baptism 29 April 1744; Jean-Baptiste, baptism 6 April 1748. Source – DNCF & TD

MARTIN – KITHI8ANNE

Jean Martin, Savage (Indian) of Acadie married Rose Kithi8anne (Indian) at Quebec 1772. She was baptised 1737, died 4 March 1773 at Baie-St-Paul. Child was Chrysosiome, baptism 3 March 1773. Source – DNCF & TD

MARTIN (OUESTNOROUEST LINE)

Jean Martin, born c. 1671, son of Pierre Martin and Anne Ouestnorouest (Indian) married 1696 to Madeleine Babin, b.c. 1678, daughter of Antoine Babin and Marie Mercier. Children were: Claire, b.c. 1697 who married #1 to Pierre Vinet and #2 Julien Plessis; Cecile, b.c. 1698 married Etienne Trunet; Anne, b.c. 1699 who married Jean-Baptiste Jehannot; Marie-Josephe, b. 1700 who married Jean Bourhis; Isabelle (Elisabeth), b.c. 1702 married Philibert Pineau; Marguerite married Jean Guilton; Jean-Baptiste, b.c. 1709; A daughter, b.c. 1707; Joseph, b.c. 1713 married Julienne Paul; Francois, b. 1715; A daughter, b. 1717; Pierre, b. 1722; Louis, b. 1724. Source – DGDFA & Census 1671

MARTIN – OUESTNOROUEST

Pierre Martin born 5 Oct. 1632 at St. Germain de Bourgueil, son of Pierre Martin and Catherine Vigneau. He was a laborer and married first in 1660 to Anne Ouestnorouest dit Petitous who was born around 1644 and died 1686. Their 9 children were: Pierre, b.c. 1661 and married Anne Godin dit Chatillon, daughter of Pierre Godin and Jeanne Pousseliere; Rene, b.c. 1663; Andre, b.c. 1666; Jacques, b.c. 1669; Jean, b.c. 1671 and married 1696 to Madeleine Babin, daughter of Antoine Babin and Marie Mercier; Cecile, b.c. 1673; a daughter (unnamed), b.c. 1675; Marie, b.c. 1678 who married 11 Feb. 1710 to Jean-Baptiste Pellerin, son of Etienne Pellerin and Jeanne Savoie; Renee, b.c. 1680.

Pierre married again in 1686 to Jeanne Rousseliere, daughter of Louis Rousseliere and Isabelle Parise. Pierre died age 69 on 11/12 Nov. 1746. (This line continues in Steve White's book if more research is needed). Anne Ouestnorouest name was refered to as Anne Petitous in her daughter Marie's marriage record of 11 Feb. 1710.

Source – DGDFA & DGDFA Eng Sup & MNH & LRAMD

MARTIN (OUESTNOROUEST LINE)

Pierre Martin, b.c. 1661, laborer and son of Pierre Martin and Anne Ouestnoouest (Indian) married 1686 to Anne Godin dit Chatillon, daughter of Pierre Godin and Jeanne Rousseliere. Anne was born in Montreal, Quebec on 10 Jan. 1672. Children were: Cecile, b.c. 1687; Renee, b.c. 1688; Madeleine, b.c. 1689; Etienne, b.c. 1691; Pierre, b.c. 1693 and married Marie-Josephe Clemenceau; Francois, b.c. 1693 who married Angelique Bertrand; Marie, b.c. 1695 who married #1 Pierre Bertaud and #2 Mathieu de Glain dit Cadet; Joseph, b. 1697 who married #1 Isabelle (Elisabeth) Carret and #2 Anne-Marie Michel; Anne, b.c. 1699 who married Marin Fortin; Angelique, b.c. 1700 who married #1 Antoine Gourdon and #2 Jean Blouet; Barthelemy who married Madeleine Carret; Marie-Madeleine, b.c. 1706; Paul, b.c. 1707 who married

Genevieve Dubois; Charles, b.c. 1709 who married Francoise Carret; Jean, b.c. 1711; A daughter, b.c. 1717; Isabelle (Elisabeth), b.c. 1716 who married #1 Diego dit Jacques Martinez and #2 Lucas (Luc) Le Metayer. Source – DGDFA

MARTIN/BARNABE – SKOKANE
Joseph Martin also known as Joseph Barnabe was born about 1801 at Quebec. Parents were, Francois Martin and Francoise Dagneau who married 4 Feb. 1799 at Saint Roch l'Achigan, Quebec. Joseph's first wife was Angelique Plante, 2nd. Wife was Marie Su-me-chay Indian daughter of ?... Spokane before 1836. They relocated in 1838 to Red River, Alberta, then he married again to Isabelle Bouche. Source – GMMF

MASSE – COUC-LAFLEUR
Michel Masse, son of Martin Masse and M. Therese David married Marguerite Couc-Lafleur, daughter of Pierre Couc-Lafleur and Marie Mite8ameg8k8e (Indian) 1702. Please refer to http://www.leveillee.net/ancestry/d294.htm#marguerite For her second marriage to Michel Massé, their children and descendants at: PRDH
http://www.leveillee.net/ancestry/famille9527.htm
Source – DNCF & LEV

MASSON - FRONSAC
Michel Masson, baptism 1706, died 8 Nov. 1757 at St-Charles, son of Michel married #1 1725 to Marie Fronac (Sauvagesse) Indian. Children were; Joseph-Marie, baptism 15 July 1726 at St-Valier; Etienne, baptism 4 Aug. 1728 at Beaumont, died 22 July 1732; Antoine, baptism 2 Nov. 1730, died 1 Oct. 1732. Michel's 2nd. Marriage 30 Sept. 1732 to Madeleine Dumont, baptism 1712, daughter of Julien. They had 12 children. Source – TD

MAUPETIT – PANISE
Gaspard Maupetit married Marie-Anne Panise (Indian) (Page 688). Source – TD

MC PHERSON – SAUVAGESSE
Mr. Mc Pherson married a Sauvagesse (Indian) 1776.
Source – DNCF & TD

MEDOSSET (AMERINDIENNE)
Marie Medosset (Medechese), an Amerindienne, born around 1653 married 1685 to Grand-Claude, another Amerindien. (I entered this marriage though they are both Native North American's because of the French surname for future descendant research to native line). (See Grand-Claude listing for family). Source – DGDFA

MEKINAC – JOUJOT
Joseph Mekinac, an Algonquin Indian married M. Louise Joujot, an Algonquin at Ste-Anne de la Perade, Quebec on 9 Jan. 1779. Source – DNCF & TD

MEMBERTOU/MEMBERTOUCICHIS
Actavdinech, 3rd. son of Henry Membertou was named Paul by sieur de Poutrincourt, after Pope Paul. Wife of Paul was Renee, named after Madame d'Ardanville. Source – JRAD

MEMBERTOU/MEMBERTOUCICHIS
Anne, niece of Henry, Monsieur de Coullongne sponsor in the name of Mademoiselle de Grandmare, after her name.
Source – JRAD

MEMBERTOU/MEMBERTOUCICHIS
Charlotte, 6th Daughter of said Louis (see his record for dates and places), Rene Matheu was godfather, named after his mother. No marriage listed. Source – JRAD

MEMBERTOU/MEMBERTOUCICHIS

Catherine, fourth daughter of Louis (see below same date and place) was baptized and named after his mother. No marriage listed. Source – JRAD

MEMBERTOU/MEMBERTOUCICHIS

Christine, age 13, daughter of Louis (listed below), was also baptized (same day and place) by same Monsieur, he named her after Madame the eldest daughter of France.
Source – JRAD

MEMBERTOU/MEMBERTOUCICHIS

Claude, 3rd daughter of said Louis (below, same date and place) was baptized and given name in honor of his wife.
Source – JRAD

MEMBERTOU/MEMBERTOUCICHIS

Elizabeth, age 11, second daughter of the listed below Louis, named by the Monsieur (Same day and place) after Madame, the youngest daughter of France. Source – JRAD

MEMBERTOU/MEMBERTOUCICHIS

Henry, possible son of Louis had wife named Marre, after the Queen by sieur de Poutrincourt. Source – JRAD

MEMBERTOU/MEMBERTOUCICHIS

Jacqueline, youngest daughter of Nicholas was named by said sieur, godfather for Jacques de Salazar, his son.
Source – JRAD

MEMBERTOU/MEMBERTOUCICHIS

Jeanne, 5th Daughter of Louis (listed here, see dates, places) named by sieur de Poutrincourt, after one of his daughters. No marriage listed. Source – JRAD

MEMBERTOU/MEMBERTOUCICHIS
Louis, one wife was named after Mme. De Sigogne, sponsor was Monieur de Joui. One other wife was named after Madame de Dampierre, sponsor was sieur de Poutrincourt.
Source – JRAD

MEMBERTOU/MEMBERTOUCICHIS
Louis Membertou, age 5 years old, eldest son of Membertoucoichis baptized 24 June (possibly 1610) at Church of Port Royal, New France on Saint John the Baptist day, by Monsieur de Poutrincourt and named John after himself.
Source – JRAD

MEMBERTOU/MEMBERTOUCICHIS
Louise, eldest daughter of Nicholas was named by said Sieur, sponsor in name of Madame de Belloy, his niece.
Source – JRAD

MEMBERTOU/MEMBERTOUCICHIS
Marguerite, daughter of Henry was named after the Queen by sieur de Poutrimcourt godfather. No marriage listed.
Source – JRAD

MEMBERTOU/MEMBERTOUCICHIS
Nicholas (Agovdegoven), cousin of Henry was named after Monsieur de Noyes, a Lawyer of the Parliament of Paris by sieur de Poutrincourt. Source – JRAD

MEMBERTOU/MEMBERTOUCICHIS
Philippe, wife of Nicholas was named by sieur de Poutrincourt godfather, in name of his nephew. Source – JRAD

MEMBERTOU/MEMBERTOUCICHIS
Robert (Amest), cousin of Henry was named after Monsieur the Nuncio, by godfather sieur de Poutrincourt.
Source – JRAD

MENARD – COUC-LEFEBVRE
Maurice Menard, son of Jacques Menard and Catherine
Fortier. Maurice was an interpreter to the Michillimakinac
who married Madeleine Couc-Lefebvre, daughter of Pierre
Couc-Lefebvre and Marie Mite8ameg8k8e (Indian) in 1692 at
Michellimakinac. Please refer to
http://www.leveillee.net/ancestry/d294.htm#menard for
verified data on Maurice and Marie Madeleine, and their
descendants.
Source – DNCF & LEV

MERVILLON – PANISE
Rene Mervillon married Marguerite Panise (Indian) (Page
688). Source – TD

METIOMEK
Jean-Baptiste Metiomek, an Algonquin, born 29 Aug. 1696 at
Montreal, Quebec. No parents listed. Source – TD

METIVIER – COUTURIER
Jean Metivier, son of Mathurin Metivier and Louise Binet of
Bourgeois married Genevieve Couturier, daughter of Jacques
Couturier and Catherine Annennontak (Indian) 31 Oct. 1701 at
Quebec. Source DNCF

MICHELLIMAKINA
Marie (Michellimakina), born 1727, died 3 Nov. 1755 at
General Hospital, M. (Montreal?), Quebec. No parents listed.
Source – TD

MICMAC (INDIAN)
Jean age 35, Micmac of Ristigouche, Acadie (New
Brunswick) (Possible baptism, no date). Source – TD

MICMAC

Marie-Ursule, Micmac, b. 4 Aug. 1692 (a l'age de 2 ans) at Quebec (Baptismal record?) Source – TD

MIGONIN

Marie-Joseph Migonin, baptized 23 May 1752 at la Baie-St-Paul, Quebec. No parents or marriage listed. Source – TD

MITEOUAMEGOUKOUE, CATHERINE

Indienne. Baptised at Trois-Rivieres, Quebec on 1 Nov. 1652. Father was Asababich (Indien) and Marie Mite8ameg8k8e (Indien). These parents also had a son, Pierre. Asababich was later murdered by Mohawks after attacking the Algonquin Village c. 1652-53, and abducted both these children along with Kateri Tekakwitha's mother.
Please refer to the verified data at
http://www.leveillee.net/ancestry/d296.htm
Catherine did not have a FAMILY NAME.
Catherine is the daughter of Asababich and Mite8ameg8k8e. She had a brother named Pierre. Asababich was Mite8ameg8k8e's first husband, who was killed during a Mohawk raid around 1652-1653, and their two children, along with other children and women, were abducted by the raiding Mohawks. Kateri Tekakwitha's mother was abducted also during this raid. Please refer to Norm Léveillée's story of Tekakwitha's mother at
http://www.leveillee.net/roots/norm5-1eng.htm and also my story about my cousin Tekakwitha at
http://www.kateritekakwitha.org/kateri/mycousin/index.html
Source – JR & LEV

MIUS – MI'KMAG (MICMAC INDIAN)
Francois Mius, born 1681 Acadie, Canada, son and Philippe
Mius and Marie (Micmac Indian) married c. 1700 to Marie, a
Micmac Indian. Children were: Jean Baptiste, born 1701
Acadie; Mathieu, born 1703 Acadie; Madeleine, born 1705
Acadie; Anne; Francoise, born 1709 Acadie; Francois, born
1711 Acadie. Source – PS

MIUS – MI'KMAG (MICMAC INDIAN)
Jean-Baptiste Mius (Parents not listed) married Marie, a
Micmac Indian. Children were: Marie-Josephte Mius who
married Charles-Amand Mius. Source – PS

MIUS (AMERINDIENNE LINE)
Joseph Mius, b.c. 1679, son of Philippe Mius and #1
Amerindienne (Indian) wife married Marie Amireau, daughter
of Francois Amireau and Marie Pitre 1699. (PS source says he
married Marie Amirault). Children were: Joseph, b.c. 1700-22
who married Marie-Josephe Prejean; Charles, b.c. 1702 who
married Marie-Marthe Hebert; Francois, b.c. 1703-22 who
married Jeanne Duon; Angelique, b.c. 1704-22 who married
Francois Grosvalet; Marie-Josephe, b.c. 1706 married Jean-
Baptiste Raymond; Claire, b.c. 1709 who married Charles Paul
Hebert; Marie-Madeleine, b.c. 1710 who married Jean-Baptiste
Henry; Jean-Baptiste, b.c. 1713 who married Marie-Joseph
Surette; Marguerite, b.c. 1716 who married #1 Michel Hebert
and #2 Jean Delage; Cecile, b.c. 1717 married Augustin dit
Justice Doucet; Genevieve, b.c. 1720 married Francois Guerin;
Rosalie, b.c. 1725 married Eloi Lejeune; Charles-Benjamin, b.c.
1728 married Marie-Josephe Guedry. Source – DGDFA & PS

MIUS – MI'KMAG (MICMAC INDIAN)
Laurent Mius, born 1749, Acadie, Canada, died 8 July 1811 at
Quinan, Acadie, son of Jean-Baptiste Mius and Marie-
Josephte Surette married Marie, a Micmac Indian. She died at
Quinan. Source – PS

MIUS – (AMERINDIENNE)
Mathieu Mius, born around 1682 son of Philippe Mius and first wife (Indian) (PS Source mother was Marie, a Mi'Kmag Indian), married around 1704 or 1706 at Cap Sable, Acadie to Marie-Madeleine, an Amerindienne (Micmac), who was born around 1706. Children were: Joachim, b.c. 1707 Cap Sable; Marie. Source – DGDFA & PS

MIUS – (AMERINDIENNE)
Maurice Mius, born around 1682, son of Philippe Mius and first wife (Indian) married Marguerite, an Amerindienne (Micmac), b.c. 1681 around 1702 in Acadie. Children were: Madeleine, b.c. 1703 at Mouscoudabouet; Marie-Josephe, b.c. 1707 at Mouscoudabouet. Source – DGDFA & PS

MIUS – (AMERINDIENNE)
Philippe Mius d'Azy, born c. 1660, Le Heve, Acadie, son of Philippe Mius and Madeleine Helie married #1 in 1678 to a non identified Amerindienne and #2 1687 to Marie, an Amerindienne. Children by first marriage were: Joseph, b.c. 1679 Cap Sable and married Marie Amireau; Marie, b.c. 1680 Cap Sable, Acadie and married Francois Viger; Maurice, b.c. 1682 and married Marguerite ?; Mathieu, b.c. 1682 Cap Sable married Marie-Madeleine ?; Francoise married Jacques Bonnevie of Beaumont. Children by 2nd Marriage: Jacques, b.c. 1688, La Heve and married unknown in 1715; Marie married Jean-Baptiste Thomas; Pierre d'Azy Mius, b.c. 1691, La Heve married Marguerite Lapierre; Madeleine, b.c. 1694, La Heve married Jean-Baptiste Guedry; Jean-Baptiste married Marie ?; Francoise, b.c. 1697, La Heve married #1 unknown, #2 Rene Grand-Claude (part Indian) and #3 Marie ? (A Micmac); Francois, b.c. 1681, La Heve married c. 1700 to Marie ?; Philippe III, b.c. 1703; Anne-Marie, b.c. 1705, La Heve married Paul Guedry.
Source – DGDFA & AMD & PS & LRAMD

MORAND – PANISE
Jean-Louis Morand married Marie-Anne Panise (Indian) (page 688). Source – TD

MORAND – SAUVAGES
Marie-Charlotte Morand married Jean-Baptiste, Sauvages. Child was Jean-Marie, baptized 28 June 1737 at Lorette, Quebec. Source – TD

MORISETTE – INDIAN
Aresene Morisette was born about 1795 at Quebec, Canada. He was Baptisted 10 April 1785 at Ste. Genevieve, Pierrefonds, Montreal, Quebec. Possible parents were Jean-Marie Morisette and Marie Agathe Guyon. Aresene married 1828 to Therese "Indian." Their Children were: Aresene; Jean Baptiste; Norbert. Source – GMMF

NAHIKIGIK8K8E
Marie Nahikigik8k8e, an Algonquine, died 28 Feb. 1699 age 80. Source – TD

NAD8E8ISCH
Marguerite Nad8e8isch, an Algonquine, b. 18 July 1695 at Montreal, Quebec. Source – TD

NAPECHE – PELLETIER
Joseph Napeche married Marie-Louise Pelletier. Child was Marie-Louise, baptized 26 Sept. 1758 at la Baie-St-Paul, Quebec. Source – TD

NASKAPIS
Francoise-Marie, Naskapis, appartenant a Michel Legardeur, baptized 19 June 1746 at Quebec. No marriage listed. Source – TD

NECTABO – AN8TGIN

Rene Nectabo married Catherine An8tgin near Port Royal, Acadie on 24 Aug. 1726. A witness was Baptiste Thomas, chief of the Indians on the river of Port Royal, Acadie. Source – DGDFA Eng Sup

NEMELO SAUVAGES

Marguerite (Nemelo) Sauvages, a Micmac baptism 7 Aug. 1701 at Quebec. No marriage listed. Source – TD

NEMIRAOUR

Joseph (Nemiraour), a Micmac, born 1701, baptized 26 July 1702 at Ste-Anne, Quebec. No parents or marriage listed. Source – TD

NICOLET – SAUVAGESSE

Jean Nicolet (1598-1642), son of Thomas Nicolet and Marguerite De La Mar of Cherbourg, Normandie, France married 1627 Nipissing Sauvagesse (Algonquin or Huron Indian) du Lac Nipissing. Found on page 994 of source. A record dated 1627 says he was Jean Nicolet de Belleborne (Metis?) born 1598, died 1642 married an Algonquian or Huron. The population of Quebec was only 67 including children. http://www.leveillee.net/ancestry/nicoletmorteng.htm has an excerpt of his death in both English and in French. Source – DNCF & MC & DGA & LEV

NIPISSINGUE

Thomas Nipissingue, baptized 7 Nov. 1712 at St-Francois, I. J. No parents listed. Source – TD

NORMAND – GAKERLENNENTA

Charles Normand (Jolicoeur), son of Pierre Normand and M. Josephte Quier married Therese Gakerlennenta (A possible Indian?) on 12 Feb. 1760 at Lac des Deux-Montagnes, Quebec. Source – DNCF

NORMAND
Francois Normand dit Ouaspoux, Metis died 1750, Quebec.
His record appears to be the first use of Metis. Source – DGA

NORMAND – MIDUNAQUEL
Louis-Francois Normand, a Metis Indian married Marguerite
Midunaquel, a Micmac Indian. Date and location not given but
listed on page 999 of source. Source – DNCF

OK8B8IN
Louis Ok8b8in, an Algonquin, born 16 Sept. 1698 at
Montreal, Quebec. Source – TD

ONDAKION – ASENRAQUEHAON
Pierre Ondakion, a Huron Indian from du bourg de la
Conception, Ontario married Jeanne Asenraquehaon, probably
another Indian. There was no date or location given, but found
on page 1002 of the source. Child was Genevieve-Agnes
Skanndharon, b. 1638. Record says in French, "hospitaliere
dite Genevieve-Agnes de tous les Saints; died 3 Nov. 1657 at
Quebec." Source – DNCF & TD

ONAQUACOMENNE – ALGONQUINE
Michel Onaquacomenne, an Algonquin Indian married
Francoise, an Algonquine Indian. Date and location not given
but found on page 1002 of source. Source – DNCF

ONONASKA
Francois (Ononaska) Sauvage, an Abenaquis, baptism 9 July
1709 at Quebec. No marriage listed. Source – TD

ONONTAGUE
Charles Onontague, born 1720, baptized 27 Aug. 1745 at
Quebec. Baptized by Mgr. DePontBriand et filleul de M. de
Beauharnais, Quebec. No marriage listed. Source – TD

ONONTAGUE
Gilles Onontague, born 1718, baptized 27 Aug. 1745 at Quebec. (Filleul de M. Hocquart). No marriage listed. Source – TD

ORI8AE
Antaine Ori8ae, one youth died 31 May 1698 at Quebec. Source – TD

OSSISSIKOPINOS
Guillaume Ossissikopinos, an Algonquin, born 2 July 1698 at Montreal, Quebec. Source – TD

OUACHESSE
Cecile-Charlotte Ouachesse, appartenant a M. Estebe, born 1723, baptized 4 May 1747 at Quebec. No marriage listed. Source – TD

OUENIMOET
Joseph (Sauvages) Ouenimoet of Becancour, died 17 Oct. 1714 at Quebec. No marriage listed. Source – TD

OULAKOUS
Agnes Oulakous, an adult (demeurant chez M.) De St. Denis, died 29 Sept. 1685 at Beauport, Quebec. Source – TD

OUTAOUIS
Marie (Outaouis), died 3 Nov. 1755 at General Hospital, M. (Montreal?), Quebec. Source – TD

OYOIC
Jean-Paul Oyoic, son of Jean-Paul and Marguerite Oyoic, baptized 12 Sept. 1723 at St-Pierre, Quebec. Source – TD

PACHIRINI, CHARLES

Algonquin, but no spouse listed at Trois-Rivieres, Quebec on 16 April 1657. The date listed here is really the date of Pierre Couc & Mite8ameg8k8e's wedding 16 Apr 1657 at which Sachem Carolus Pachirini served as a witness. Charles was the chief of the Algonquin clan at Trois-Rivières. Please refer to http://www.leveillee.net/ancestry/pachirini.htm There is information there about him, his two wives (no dates) and his several children. There is also a reference to him, correcting René Jetté's error in regard to Mite8ameg8k8e at http://www.leveillee.net/ancestry/d296.htm Source – JR & LEV

PACHIRINICH – PAKINTEMDAMAGES

Jean Pachirinich and Francoise Pakintemdamages Amerindian son, Mathurin was the godson of Mathurin Landry on 29 July 1643. Paul Lejeune, S.J., one of the founders of the mission at Trios-Rivieres, Quebec poured the baptismal waters on the forehead of the Indian child. Source – OFCA – XI

PAGE – OBOMSAWIN (AT ODANAK)

Adeline Page, daughter of Etienne Page and Euphrosine Dulier married Louis Obomsawin (at Odanak) (Abinaki Indian line?) (Ref. Luce Portneuf) 22 Nov. 1853 Source – MSQ

PAKEKANAK8SKAN - PAPISKANA8A

Louise, born 27 July 1697 at Montreal, Quebec, daughter of ?... Pakekanak8skan and Marguerite Papiskana8a, an Algonquine. Source – TD

PANIS

Noel Panis, baptized 25 Dec. 1719 at Lachine, Quebec. No parents listed. Source – TD

PANIS
Philippe-Marie-Louise Panis, born 9 June 1696, age 15 years at Montreal, Quebec, amenee en Canada par M. Daillebout de Coulonge, et filleule de Philippe De Rigaut de Vaudreuil. Source – TD

PAPINOCHOIS
Richard Papinochois, baptized 29 June 1697 at la Baie-St-Paul, Quebec. No parents or marriage listed. Source – TD

PARISIEN – SAUVAGESSE
Jean Parisien married Francoise Sauvagesse (Indian). No date or location given, but listed on page 1031 of source. Tanguay says child was, Mathurin b. 1641, baptisted 1644 at Trois-Rivieres, Quebec. Source – DNCF & TD

PATAK
Marie-Agnes Patak, appartenant au sieur Lamotte, medecin, baptized 1732, died 6 Feb. 1748 at Lachenaye. No parents listed. Source – TD

PELLERIN – MARTIN (OUESTNOROUEST LINE)
Jean-Baptiste Pellerin, b.c. 1685, son of Etienne Pellerin and Jeanne Savoie married 11 Feb. 1710 to Marie Martin, daughter of Pierre Martin and Anne Ouestnorouest (Indian) dit Petitous. Children were: Marguerite, b.c. 1711 who married Claude Doucet; Pierre, b.c. 1713; Marie, b.c. 1715 who married Jacques Raymond; Pierre, b.c. 1717 who married Anne Girouard; Jean-Baptiste, b.c. 1719 who married Marie-Josephe Bourg; Agathe, b.c. 1723. Source – DGDFA

PELLETIER (ALGONQUIN) – DAUZA-ALGONKINE
Antoine Pelletier (Algonquin), son of Michel Pelletier and Francoise Meneux married 1721 Marie Dauza-Algonkine (Both Algonquine Indians?). Date and location not given, but listed on page 1040 of source. Antoine's father and mothers

marriage record does not state that they are Indian.
Please refer to PRDH file at
http://www.leveillee.net/ancestry/union7848.htm
There are many PELLETIER ancestors in my site. Check out
the Index at
http://www.leveillee.net/ancestry/fowndx.htm#PELLETIER
Source - DNCF & TD & LEV & PRDH

PELLETIER - ISKUAMISKUSKUEU
Charles Pelletier, son of Nicolas Pelletier married 7 Feb. 1720
at Chicoutimi, Quebec to Marie-Madeleine Iskuamiskuskueu.
Source – FQM

PELLETIER – AMERINDIENNE
Francois Pelletier, born c. 1635, St. Pierre de Galardon,
Chartres, France, son of Nicolas (Antaya) Pelletier and Jeanne
Voissy (Roussy). He died between 14 May 1690 and 9 July
1697, Dautray, Quebec. He married 1660, Quebec to Dorothee
Amerindienne (Indian) who was possibly born in Quebec,
Canada and died before 26 Sept. 1661 (13 April 1661 at
Quebec), Quebec, Canada. It is told that they had no children.
Source – DRU & DNCF & GMMF & TD

PELLETIER – SAUVAGESSE
Nicolas Pelletier married Marie Sauvagesse (Indian), daughter
of Grand Chief Jean-Baptiste Nanabesa 5 August 1715 at
Quebec. Source – DNCF & TD

PELLETIER – TEGOUSSI
Nicolas Pelletier (Peltier)(Marolles), son of Nicolas Pelletier
and Jeanne De Voissy of Commis married Madeleine
Tegoussi, a Montagnaise (Indian) 22 June 1673 at Quebec.
Source – DNCF

PETITPAS – (AMERINDIENNE)

Claude Petitpas, born around 1663, died 1731, son of Claude Petitpas and Catherine Bugaret was a Captain de goelette, interpreter and merchant married Marie-Therese, b.c. 1668, died 1717 an Amerindienne around 1668 in Acadie. Children were: Barthelemy, b.c. 1687 River Miramichi, New Brunswick married Madeleine Coste; Judith, b.c 1693 married Bernard Marres; Paul, b.c. 1695; Joseph, b.c. 1699; Marie-Louise, b.c. 1701 married Louis Moyse; Isidore, b.c. 1703; Francoise, b.c. 1706 married Jacques dit Jacob Coste.
Source – DGDFA & AMD & LRAMD

PHILIPPE – NEPTON

Ludger Nepton (Abenaki Indian), son of John-Baptiste Nepton and Marguerite Vincent married Marie Neptona Philippe 1 Sept. 1880 at Becancour, Quebec. Source – MBQ

PI8AKAMIGAN

Marie-Josette Pi8akamigan, an Algonquin, born 9 June 1697 at Montreal, Quebec, died 12 June 1697. Source – TD

PICHARD – PADOKA

Louis Pichard married Marie-Anne Padoka (Indian) (page 688). Source – TD

PISNET (AMERINDIENNE)

Pierre Pisnet an Amerindien of Cap Sable, Acadie, married 1706 to Anne ? Children were: Marie, b.c. 1707 who married Francois Doucet, son of Germain Doucet and Francoise ?
Source – DGDFA & AMD

PIXISCHET8ILLANT

Jean-Baptiste, Tete-de-Boule of Chicoutimi, son of Jean-Baptiste Pixischet8illant, born 1775, baptized 24 Dec. 1778 at Ste-Anne-de-la-Perade, Quebec. No marriage listed.
Source – TD

PLAISANCHE
Francois Plaisanche, a Montagnais married Francoise, a Micmac on 2 June 1719 at Ste-Anne, Quebec. Children were, Marie-Victoire, baptized 22 Oct. 1724, Martin, baptized 23 July 1725. Source – TD

POISSON (INDIAN)
Ignace Blanc Poisson, born 26 June 1687 at Cape de la Madeleine. Source – TD

POLICHISH
Marie-Louise Polichish, an Algonquine, died 14 Feb. 1690 at Montreal, Quebec. Source – TD

POLLET – PELLETIER
Louis Pollet, son of Hilaire Pollet and Francoise Signoret of d'Azay, diocese of Pottiers, Potiou, France married Marie Pelletier, daughter of Nicolas Pelletier and Marie Sauvagesse (Indian) 9 Jan. 1739 at Quebec. Source – DNCF

PORTNEUF - ABENAQUISE
Jean-Baptiste Portneuf married Marie-Anne Abenaquise (Indian). Source – TD

PREVOST – CADIEU
Jean Prevost, son of Martin Prevost and M. Olivier-Silvestre Manithabehick (Indian) married Francoise Cadieu, daughter of Charles Cadieu and Michelle-Madeleine Macard 4 May 1690 at Quebec. Source – DNCF

PREVOST – SEDILOT
Jean-Baptiste Prevost, son of Martin Prevost and M. Olivier-Silvestre Manithabehick (Indian) married M. Genevieve Sedilot, daughter of Jean Sedilot and M. Claire De La Hogue 3 Feb. 1712 at Ste. Foy, Quebec. Source – DNCF

PREVOST – GIROU

Jean-Baptiste Prevost, son of Martin Prevost and M. Olivier-Silvestre Manithabehick (Indian) married Marie Girou, daughter of Toussaint Girou and Marie Godard 18 Aug. 1683 at Beauport, Quebec. Source – DNCF

PREVOST – CAREAU

Louis Prevost, son of Martin Prevost and M. Olivier-Silvestre Manithabehick (Indian) married Marguerite Careau, daughter of Louis Careau and Jeanne Lerouge 17 Feb. 1681 at Chateau-Richer, Quebec. He is listed again as marrying Francoise Gagnon, daughter of Mathurin Gagnon and Francoise Gideau 21 Feb. 1672 at Chateau-Richer, Quebec. Source – DNCF

PREVOST – GIROUX

Louis Prevost, son of Louis Prevost (Whose mother was Indian) and Marguerite Careau married M. Anne Giroux, daughter of Raphael Giroux and Madeleine Vachon 9 July 1731 at Quebec. Louis Prevost has another marriage to M. Therese Maheu, daughter of Pierre Maheu and M. Louise Garnier 7 Nov. 1712 at Beauport, Quebec. Source – DNCF

PREVOST/PROVOST LINES

For all the below listed please refer to the list of names at http://www.leveillee.net/ancestry/fowndx.htm#PROVOST Also, links from that page to Martin. Source – LEV

PROVOST/PREVOST – MANITOUBEWICH

Marin/Martin Prevost/Provost was born 4 Jan. 1611, Montreuil-sous-Bois, Vincennes, lle-de, France. Son of Pierre Prevost and Charlotte Vie (Vien/Vei). Martin married at Notre-Dame, Quebec, Quebec 3 Nov. 1644 Marie Olivier-Silvestre Manithabenhick/Manitoubewich/Manitouabeouich (Indian) who was born 1625 or 1620 and from Roch et Sauvagesse, Quebec, Canada or at St-Andre, Kamouraska, Quebec and died 10 Sept. 1665 in Quebec and buried 12 Sept.

1665 in Cimetiere de Quebec, Quebec. She was from the Huron/Huronne Nation or ...? Her parents were Roch Manitouabeouich and Outchibahabanouk Oueou. Martin died 26 Jan. 1691 at Batiscan, Quebec. The Laforest book states Marie Olivier was Amerindian and had 9 children who were born at Montreuil-sous-Bois. Tanguay listed them as: Marie-Madeleine, b. 28 Dec. 1647 who married #1 ?, and #2 11 June 1670 to Michel Aubin at Ste Famille, Quebec; Ursule, b. 14 Dec. 1649, d. 2 Jan. 1661; Louis, b. 1651, married #1 21 Feb. 1672 to Francoise Gagnon at Chateau-Richer, Quebec, #2 17 Feb. 1681 to Marguerite Careau, died 27 May 1686 at Beauport, Quebec; Jean-Baptiste, married #1 18 August 1683 to Marie Girou, #2 3 Feb. 1712 to Genevieve Sedilot at Ste. Foye; Marie-Madeleine, b. 13 Jan. 1655, d. 16 March 1661; Antoine, b. 23 Oct. 1657, d. 16 March 1661; Jean, b. 14 Feb. 1660, married Francoise Leblanc; Jean-Baptiste, b. 24 June 1662, married 4 May 1690 to Francoise Cadieu; Therese, b. 3 June 1665, married 18 August 1683 to Michel Giroux.
Source – DRU & OFCA – XI & TD

PREVOST – LESIEGE-LUCARGAVE
Pierre Prevost, son of Louis Prevost (Whose line come from an Indian) and M. Therese Maheu married Marie Lesiege-Lucargave, daughter of Etienne Lesiege-Lucargave and Francoise Bergeron 21 April 1751 at Lavaltrie, Quebec.
Source – DNCF

PREVOST – DENEAU
Raphael Prevost, son of Louis Prevost (Whose line come from an Indian) and M. Anne Giroux married Ursule Deneau, daughter of Francois-Xavier Deneau and Marie Supernant 11 Aug. 1760 at St. Constant, Quebec. Source – DNCF

PREVOST – VESINA
Vincent Prevost, son of Louis Prevost (From Indian line) and
Marguerite Careau married Agnee Vesina, daughter of
Francois Vesina and Jeanne Marie 7 Nov. 1701 at Ange-
Gardien, Quebec. Source – DNCF

RANGER – SAGOLA
Claude Ranger marriage to Felicite Sagola (Indian) (Page
688). Source – TD

REHEL – SAUVAGESSE
Julien Rehel, son of Yves Rehel and Jeanne Foure of Megrit,
diocese of St. Malo, Bretagne married Madeleine-Alexandre
Sauvagesse (Indian). Date and place not given but is listed on
page 1140 in source. Source – DNCF & TD

RENARD
Genevieve-Gabrielle Renard, appartenant a M. de Beaucourt,
Govenor of Montreal, Quebec, baptized 21 Nov. 1740 at
Quebec. No marriage listed. Source – TD

RENARD
Gilles-Hyacinthe Renard, born 1718, baptized 24 May 1738 at
Quebec. No marriage listed. Source – TD

RENARD (SAUVAGES)
Jacques Renard (Sauvages), appartenant a M. Demeule,
baptism 1700,death 15 Feb. 1717 at Quebec. Source – TD

RENARD - SAUVAGES
Jacques Renard, baptism 1709, Death 13 Feb. 1715 at Quebec.
Source – TD

RENARD
Jean-Baptiste Renard, born 1721, baptized 20 May 1741 at
Quebec. (Baptized at Veille de la Pentecote). No marriage
listed. Source – TD

RENARD (SAUVAGES)
Louise-Angelique-Catherine Renard (Sauvages), appartenant a
M. Guillaume Gaillard, conseiler, born 1702, baptism 9 July
1719 at Quebec. Source – TD

RENARD (SAUVAGES)
Louise-Genevieve Renard, born 1708, baptism 26 Nov. 1713
at Quebec. No marriage listed. Source – TD

RENARD (SAUVAGES)
Marie-Anne, Renard (Sauvages), born 1707, baptism 26 Nov.
1713 at Quebec. No marriage listed. Source – TD

RENARD (SAUVAGES)
Marie-Jeanne Renard (Sauvages), born 1703, baptism 14 Nov.
1716 at Quebec. No marriage listed. Source – TD

RENARD
Marie-Joseph Renard, born 1705, baptized 1741 at Quebec.
No marriage listed. Source – TD

RENARD
Marie-Louise Renard, appartenant a Francois Dupont, born
1731, baptized 8 July 1738 at Quebec. Died 14 July 1741.
Source – TD

RENARD (SAUVAGES)
Marie-Louise (Sauvages) Renard, apptenant a M. Vaudreuil,
gouverneur du Canada, born 1688, baptiste 13 Dec. 1723 at
Quebec. Source – TD

RENARD
Marguerite-Genevieve (Sauvages) Renard, appartenant a M.
Vaudrauil, gouverneur du Canada, born 1709, baptism 13 Dec.
1723 at Quebec. Source – TD

RENARD
Marie-Anne Renard, appartenant a Jacques Philibert, born
1722, baptized 29 Feb. 1740 at Quebec. No marriage listed.
Source – TD

RENARD (SAUVAGES
Marie-Madeleine Renard (Sauvages), born 1709, baptism 1
Oct. 1714 at Quebec. No marriage listed. Source – TD

RENARD (SAUVAGES)
Marie-Philippe (Sauvages) Renard, born 1684, baptism 17th.
And death 18 Dec. 1729 at Quebec. Source – TD

RENARD (SAUVAGES)
Nicolas Renard (Sauvages), achete par M. Louis Parant, apres
la defaite des Renards, born 1725, baptism 11 Jan. 1731 at
Quebec. Source – TD

RENARD (SAUVAGES)
Pierre-Denis Renard (Sauvages), achete par M. Denis-Charles
Duplessis, born 1724, baptism 28 Dec. 1730 at Quebec.
Source – TD

RENARD (SAUVAGES)
Pierre-Francois Renard (Sauvages), born 1706, baptism 12
Oct. 1714 at Quebec. No marriage listed. Source – TD

RENARD
Pierre-Joseph Renard, appartenant a Pierre Rodrigue, born
1742, baptized 9 Nov. 1746 at Quebec. No marriage listed.
Source – TD

RENARD
Marie-Anne Renard, a servant of M. De la Morille, born 1704, died 24 Oct. 1727 at Quebec. Source – TD

RENARD
Marie-Francoise Renard, born 1727, baptized 6 April 1733 at Quebec. Source – TD

RENAUD – AMERINDIENNE
Jean Renaud dit Bordenave, b.c. 1652 married 1687 to an unnamed Amerindienne at Pentagouet, Quebec. They had 4 children all listed unnamed in 1693 records.
Source – DGDFA & DGDFA Eng Sup

RENAUD
Jean-Baptiste Renaud, a Micmac, baptized 1687, died (trouve gele) 9 Feb. 1767 at la Baie-St-Paul, Quebec. No parents or marriage listed. Source – TD

RHEAUME – OUAOUAGOUKOUE
Jean-Baptiste Rheaume , born 1675, married Symphorose Ouaouagoukoue (Indian) 1 June 1720, possibly Quebec. Source – Metis

RHODES – SAUVAGESSE
Gerard Rhodes married a Marie Sauvagesse (Indian). There is no name, date or place listed, but is on page 1148 of the source. Source – DNCF & TD

RICARA
Jean-Baptiste (Ricara), baptized 15 July 1718 at Lachine, died 19 Oct. 1718. No parents listed. Source – TD

RICHARD
Marguerite Richard, a Micmac, baptized 25 Feb. 1720 at Ste-Anne, Quebec. No parents or marriage listed. Source – TD

RIVAL – SAUVAGESSE

Ignace Rival married Marie Sauvagesse (Indian). No date or placed listed but can be entry is on page 1157 of source. Source – DNCF & TD

ROBILLARD – SCATCHI8C8A

Adrien Robillard/Robillard, born 9 Oct. 1679 at Champlain, son of Claude Robillard and Marie Binard (Parents married 1678) married Domitilde Scatchi8c8a, an Illinoise Indian. No date or location reference in source DNCF page 1170. He died 4 Jan. 1721 at Kaskakia, Quebec.

Adrien was not the son of Marie Binard, but of Marie Grandin, the second wife of Claude Robillard. Marie Grandin was a "fille du roi". Please refer to:

http://www.leveillee.net/ancestry/robillard/d5rob8.htm
And the reference from PRDH
http://www.leveillee.net/net/ancestry/union4046.htm
The PRDH document for SCATCHI8C8A makes no mention of her origins. However, the name is surely Native American (the "8" in Algonquin and the French equivalent "ou" indicate that).
http://www.leveillee.net/ancestry/fillesduroi4.htm#grandin
Source – DNCF & TD & LEV & PRDH

ROBIN (LATOUCHE) – ROY

Jean Robin (Latouche), son of Jean Robin and Jeanne Gadolet of Chaniers, diocese of Saintes, Saintonge, France married Marguerite Roy, daughter of Pierre Roy and Madeleine Ouabanquiquois (Indian) 27 April 1739 at Quebec.
Source – DNCF

ROCHEVILLE - ALGONQUINE

Nicolas Rocheville married Marguerite Algonquine. Child was: Marie-Therese, b. 18 Oct. 1711 at Trois-Rivieres, Quebec. Source – TD

ROY (AMERINDIENNE) – CLEMENCEAU

Anne Roy, b.c. 1686, daughter of Jean Roy and Marie Aubois (Amerindienne) married 1705 at Boston, Mass. to Jean Clemenceau, son of Martial Clemenceau and Anne Duranteau. He was a sergent in the royal regiment. Children were: Marie-Josephe, b. 7 May 1706 who married Pierre Martin, son of Pierre Martin and Anne Godin; Anne, b.c. 21 Feb. 1708 married Charles Heon; Marie-Anne, b.c. 15 Feb. 1710 married Nicolas Lavigne; Louis, b.c. 26 April-8 June 1712 married Anne Caissie; Jean, b.c. 1714; Marguerite, b.c. 1717 married Jean-Baptiste Lejeune. Source – DGDFA

ROY – AUBOIS/DUBOIS (AMERINDIENNE)

Jean Roy dit Laliberte possibly born 1651 at St. Malo married 1686 to Marie (Christine) Aubois (Dubois), b.c. 1665 an Amerindienne. Children were: Anne, b.c. 1686 married at Boston to Jean Clemenceau; Marie, b.c. 1689 married #1 Joseph Comeau and #2 Mr. Girouard; Jean, b.c. 1691 married #1 Jeanne Lejeune and #2 Francoise Corporon; Francois, b.c. 1692 married Marie Bergeron; Philippe, b.c. 1696 who married Cecile Mazerolle; Charles, b.c. 1698; Marie-Madeleine, b.c. 1701 married Louis Fontaine; Marie-Francoise, b.c. 1703 married Etienne Trahan; Rene, b.c. 1708 married Marie-Josephe Daigre. Source – DGDFA & AMD & MNH & LRAMD

ROY – MINET (AMERINDIENNE)

Charles Roy, b.c. 1754, Dunstable, Mass? Son of Jean Roy and 2nd wife Francoise Corporon who were married 1743 married Louise Minet, an Amerindienne de la River Rouge on 15 Feb. 1802. Source – DGDFA

ROY/LEROY – OSKINANOTAME

Joseph Roy/LeRoy, born 1744 at Charlesbourg, Quebec, died 1825. Son of Joseph LeRoy and Marie-Louise Gagnon. He married Marguerite Oskinanotame (b. 1760 d. 1835). She was the daughter of Menominee chief Ahkenepaweh Akeeneebaway or Standing Earth and Waupanokiew. Marguerite was the granddaughter of Shawano and related to Oshkosh, Onaugesa, Kaushkaumoweh (Grizzly Bear) and Pottawattomie chief Anaugesa. Joseph and Marguerite's children were: Susan Sowankien who married Domanick Brunette; Francois (1784) who married Therese Lecuyer; Charlotte (1785) who married Joseph Campinne/Camanne in 1807; Angelique-Angeline (b. 1786/89 d. 1862) who married Jacques-Jean Vieaux Jr. in 1786; Catherine Songbird (b. 1787) who married 1st Alexis Gardapier and 2nd Joseph H. Rioux; Marie who married Jean Marie Ducharme; Pierre (b.c. 1793. Joseph was the brother of Amable Roy who married the daughter of Augustin Langlade and lived in Green Bay, Wisconsin. Source – RG

ROY/LEROY – OUANKIKOVE/OUABANKIKNOUE

Pierre Roy/LeRoy, son of Pierre Roy/LeRoy and Catherine Ducharme was born 1676 and died 1743. He married 1st. to Marguerite Ouankikove/Ouankiknoue, from the nation of Miamie (Miami/Minmis) in 1703 at Detroit, Michigan. She died 31 Oct. 1732. Their children were: Marguerite Roy/LeRoy, born 27 April 1704 and died 1755. She married Jean Robin dit Latouche in 1739; Pierre, b. 21 April 1706; Marie-Louise, b. 19 May 1708 who married 6 Jan. 1735 to Alexis Desruisseaux and died 3 Dec. 1735; Marie-Madeleine, b. 25 May 1710, married 25 May 1728 to Pierre Chesne and died 20 Nov. 1732; Francois, b. 20 April 1713; Marie-Louise, b. 3 June 1717. Pierre's 2nd. Marriage was to Marie-Angelique Faye-Lafaillette in 1705 (This date would make some of above children questionable unless DuRoy is someone else?) at Laprairie. Also listed as Pierre Du Roy. Source – RG & DNCF &DGA & TD

ROY – MACOUTENTIAOUE
Pierre Roy who died 1721 married Marie-Anne Macoutentiaoue at Kaskaskia, Illinois around 1716. She is a possible Native American. Their children were: Marie-Louise, born 1717; Genevieve, b. 1719, d. 1721. All events were at Kaskaskia, Illinois. Source – RG

ROY - OUABANQUIQUOIS
Pierre Roy married Madeleine Ouabanquiquois of the Miamis Nation. He died 31 Oct. 1732 at Detroit. They had a daughter, Marguerite, born 27 April 1704 who married 27 April 1739 to Jean Robin at Quebec. She died 21 April 1755. (This is most likely the same family as above Pierre, son of Pierre and Catherine. Source – TD

SABOURIN - 8ATAGAMIE
Jean Baptiste Sabourin married Marie-Joseph 8atagamie before 1718. Child was Pierre, born 16 March 1719 at Bout-de-l'Ile, M., Quebec Source – TD

SADAUZANTE (INDIAN) – LAMANEL
Eustache Sadouzante married Catherine Lamanel. Child was Anne, baptized 28 July 1726 at Ste-Anne, Quebec. Source – TD

SALES (SAVAGE)
Francois De Sales, enfant savage, b. 1 Oct. 1688 at Quebec. (Baptism record?) Source – TD

SASSAKI8ISECH
Pierre Sassaki8isech, an Algonquin, died 23 Sept. 1698 at Montreal, Quebec. Source – TD

SAUVAGES
Two infants of St-Francois-de-Sales, Quebec. No other information listed. Source – TD

SAUVAGES

Agnes, born Aug. 1707, baptized 8 Nov. 1707 at Ste-Anne, Quebec. No parents or marriage listed. Source – TD

SAUVAGES

Alexandre Sauvages, a Patocas, achete par M. Bondy, born 1725, baptism 8 April 1731 at Quebec. Source – TD

SAUVAGES

Ambroise Sauvages, an Abenaquis, baptism 16 July 1710 at Quebec. No marriage listed. Source – TD

SAUVAGES

Andre Sauvages, an Abenaquis, baptism 8 July 1710 at Quebec. No marriage listed. Source – TD

SAUVAGES

Angelique, born 1727, baptized 16 April 1740 at Quebec. No marriage listed. Source – TD

SAUVAGES

Angelique, baptized 1694, died 7 May 1712 at Ste-Anne, Quebec. Parents not listed. Source – TD

SAUVAGES

Angelique Sauvages, an Abenaquise, baptism 25 July 1711 at Quebec. No marriage listed. Source – TD

SAUVAGES

Angelique, a Micmac, baptized 24 Nov. 1704 at Ste-Anne, Quebec. No parents or marriage listed. Source – TD

SAUVAGES

Angelique, baptized 10 Dec. 1758 at St-Joseph, Beauce, Quebec. No parents or marriage listed. Source – TD

SAUVAGES
Angelique, du Missouri Indian, appartenant a M. Lemaitre-Lamorille, born 1721, baptized 16 Jan. 1746 at Quebec. No marriage listed. Source – TD

SAUVAGES
Angelique, an Abenaquise, baptized 4 Aug. 1737 at Quebec. No marriage listed. Source – TD

SAUVAGES
Angelique-Joseph, a Huron, baptized 26 Aug. 1748 at Quebec. No marriage listed. Source – TD

SAUVAGES
Anne-Claire, a Montagnaise Indian, born 1720, baptized 20 May 1741 at Quebec. No marriage listed. Source – TD

SAUVAGES
Anne-Marie, a Micmac, born 1740, died 10 August 1747 at Quebec. Source – TD

SAUVAGES
Anonyme, baptized and died 13 March 1763 at Ste-Anne-de-la-Perade, Quebec. No parents listed. Source – TD

SAUVAGES
Antoine, appartenant a M. Lamorille, born 1727, died 26 April 1736 at Quebec. No marriage listed. Source – TD

SAUVAGES
Antoinette-Catherine, a Brochet Indian, appartenant a M. Arguin-Yves, born 1735, baptized 30 June 1743 a Quebec. No marriage listed. Source – TD

SAUVAGES
Agathe, born 1656, died 6 Jan. 1716 at Ste-Anne-de-la-
Pocatiere, Quebec. No parents listed. Source – TD

SAUVAGES
Agathe, a Panise, appartenant a M. Duplessis, born 1717,
baptized 15 Oct. 1745 at Quebec. No marriage listed.
Source – TD

SAUVAGES
Agnes, an Abenaquise, baptized 1759, died 28 Feb. 1761 at
St-Joseph, Beauce, Quebec. No parents listed. Source – TD

SAUVAGES
Agnes, an Abenaquise of Acadie, baptized 1769, died 12
March 1774 at St-Joseph, Beauce, Quebec. No parents listed.
Source – TD

SAUVAGES
Athanase, an Abenaquis, born 1765, baptized 15 June 1772 at
St-Joseph, Beauce, Quebec. No parents listed. Source – TD

SAUVAGES
Athanase, an Abenaquis Indian, baptized 21 Aug. 1745 at
Quebec. No marriage listed. Source – TD

SAUVAGES
Augustin of Temiskaming, born 1781, baptized 29 July 1785
at Lachenaye. No parents listed. Source – TD

SAUVAGES
Augustin, de la mer de l'ouest, born 1741, baptized 24 Oct.
1746 at Ste-Anne-de-la-Perade, Quebec. No marriage listed.
Source – TD

SAUVAGES
Augustin, appartenant a M. De la Borde, born 1715, died 1
June 1724 at Quebec. Source – TD

SAUVAGES
Augustin-Joseph Sauvage, a Panis, appartenant a M. Claude
Legris, born 1714, baptiste 26 Jan. 1721 at Quebec.
Source – TD

SAUVAGES
Augustin Sauvages, an Abenaquis, baptism 21 Dec. 1703 at
Quebec. No marriage listed. Source – TD

SAUVAGES
Barbe, appartenant a M. Roma, born 1723, died 8 July 1748 at
Quebec. No marriage listed. Source – TD

SAUVAGES
Barthelemi Sauvages, appartanant au sieur Desaunier-
Desruisseaux, born 1742, died 6 May 1755 at Quebec.
Source – TD

SAUVAGES
Benoit, an Abenaquis, baptized 8 June 1762 at St-Joseph,
Beauce, Quebec. No parents listed. Source – TD

SAUVAGES
Bernard, an Abenaquis, baptized 1726, died 30 Jan. 1761 at
St-Joseph, Beauce, Quebec. No marriage or parents listed.
Source – TD

SAUVAGES
Brigitte of Becancour, baptized 1710 married Etienne …..? an
Abenaquis, died 15 Oct. 1733 at St-Augustin, Quebec.
Source – TD

SAUVAGES
Catherine, an Abenaquise, baptized 1704, died 6 Nov. 1709 at
Ste-Foye, Quebec. No parents listed. Source – TD

SAUVAGES
Catherine, an Esquimaux, appartenant a M. Bissot, born 1719,
baptized 10 August 1734 and died 22 Sept. 1734 at Quebec.
Source – TD

SAUVAGES
Catherine, a Siouse, appartenant of M. Pierre Hertel of Beau-
Bassin (New Brunswick?), born 1745, baptized 20 April 1760
at Ste-Anne-de-la-Perade, Quebec. No marriage listed.
Source – TD

SAUVAGES
Catherine-Antoinette, born 1735, died 11 July 1744 at Quebec.
Source – TD

SAUVAGES
Cecile Sauvage, a Micmac, baptism 1 Nov. 1728 at Quebec.
Source – TD

SAUVAGES
Charles, a Panis, baptized 1682, died 14 April 1703 at St-
Laurent, Quebec. Source – TD
SAUVAGES
Charles, baptized 1694, died 1 Sept. 1707 at Ste-Anne,
Quebec. (Demeurail chez Pierre Poulin). Source – TD

SAUVAGES
Charles, born 1734, baptized 11 Nov. 1748 at Quebec. No
marriage listed. Source – TD

SAUVAGES
Charles-Michel Sauvages, a Panis, born 1709, baptism 14 Oct. 1717 at Quebec. Source – TD

SAUVAGES
Charles, a Montagnais, born 1733, died 14 Nov. 1748 at Quebec. Source – TD

SAUVAGES
Charles of Lac-des-Deux-Montagnes, baptized 15 July 1770 at St-Joseph, Beauce, Quebec. No parents listed. Source – TD

SAUVAGES
Charles, baptized 26 March 1709 at St-Pierre, Quebec. Source – TD

SAUVAGES
Charles Sauvages, an Abenaquis, baptism 5 Oct. 1693 at Quebec. No marriage listed. Source – TD

SAUVAGES
Charles-Antoine Sauvages, appartenant a M. Guillemin, born 1729, baptized 22 July 1736 at Quebec. No marriage listed. Source – TD

SAUVAGES
Charles-Francois, a Micmac, baptized 6 Nov. 1730 at Kamouraska, Quebec. No parents listed. Source – TD

SAUVAGES
Charles-Francois, an Abenaquis, baptized 28 Dec. 1709 at Pte-aux-Trembles, Quebec. No marriage listed. Source – TD

SAUVAGES
Charles-Joseph, baptized 1 Jan. 1742 at Quebec. No marriage listed. Source – TD

SAUVAGES

Charlotte, baptized 1735, died 10 May 1749 at Riviere-Ouelle, Quebec. No parents listed. Source – TD

SAUVAGES

Charlotte Sauvages, appartenant a Mnn Turpin, died 8 Aug. 1761 at Quebec. Source – TD

SAUVAGES

Charlotte Sauvages, of Medoctet, baptism 11 Sept. 1707 at Quebec. No marriage listed. Source – TD

SAUVAGES

Charlotte, appartenant a M. Arguin, born 1721, died 10 August 1736 at Quebec. Source – TD

SAUVAGES

Christine, appartenant a Delle Philibert, born 1722, died 19 Feb. 1748 at Quebec. No marriage listed. Source – TD

SAUVAGES

Claire (Piscone), a Montagnaise Indian, appartenant a M. Volant, born 1721, baptized 15 Sept. 1743 at Quebec. Parents listed as Jean Tache and Claire Joliet. No marriage listed for daughter Claire. Source – TD

SAUVAGES

Claire, a Micmac, born 1730, died 15 July 1746 at Quebec. Source – TD

SAUVAGES

Constance Sauvage, an Abenaquise, baptism 1708, death 31 Jan. 1710 at Quebec. Source – TD

SAUVAGES
Domitilde, baptized 1659, died 31 Aug. 1759 at Becancour.
No parents listed. Source – TD

SAUVAGES
Domitilde Sauvages, an Abenaquise, baptism 1693, died 4
March 1701 at Quebec. Source – TD

SAUVAGES
Elisabeth, an Abenaquise, baptized 8 Jan. 1763 at St-Joseph,
Beauce, Quebec. No parents listed. Source – TD

SAUVAGES
Elisabeth, appartenant a M. Lafontaine, born 1727, died 4
April 1741 at Quebec. Source – TD

SAUVAGES (LARCHE?)
Elisabeth-Louise, a Montagnaise, adopted by Denis Larche,
born 1740, baptized 25 Jan. 1751 at Quebec. No marriage
listed. Source – TD

SAUVAGES
Etienne of Trois-Rivieres, Quebec, baptized 17 May 1765 at la
Baie-St-Paul, Quebec. No parents or marriage listed.
Source – TD

SAUVAGES
Etienne, an Abenaquis, baptiszed 1710, died 30 Oct. 1760 at
St-Joseph, Beauce, Quebec. No parents or marriage listed.
Source – TD

SAUVAGES
Etienne, an Amalecite, baptized 2 Jan. 1735 at Kamouraska,
Quebec. No parents listed. Source – TD

SAUVAGES
Etienne Sauvages, an Abenaquis, baptism 14 July 1726 at
Quebec. No marriage listed. Source – TD

SAUVAGES
Etienne-Ignace Sauvages, an Abenaquis, baptism 15 Aug.
1727 at Quebec. Source – TD

SAUVAGES
Etienne Sauvages, born Feb. 1704, baptism 21 Aug. 1704 at
Quebec. No marriage listed. Source – TD

SAUVAGES
Felicite, born March and died 9 August 1747 at Quebec.
Source – TD

SAUVAGES
Francois, baptized 1708, died 7 March 1718 at St-Pierre,
Quebec. Source – TD

SAUVAGES
Francois Sauvages, a Panis, baptism 1697, death 7 Feb. 1717
at Quebec. Source – TD

SAUVAGES
Francois Sauvages, a Panis, appartenant a Jean-Baptiste
L'Archeveque-Grand-Pre, born 1706, baptiste 5 April 1720 at
Quebec. Source – TD

SAUVAGES
Francois Sauvages, born 1730, baptized 5 Jan. 1736 at
Quebec. No marriage listed. Source – TD

SAUVAGES
Francois Sauvages, an Abenaquis, baptism 6 Oct. 1709 at
Quebec. No marriage listed. Source – TD

SAUVAGES
Francois Sauvages, an Algonquin, born Jan. 1706, baptism 17 June 1706 at Quebec. No marriage listed. Source – TD

SAUVAGES
Francois, appartenant a M. Lambert, born 1730, died 10 April 1736 at Quebec. No marriage listed. Source – TD

SAUVAGES
Francois, an Abenaquis, died 14 June 1715 at Ste-Anne, Quebec. No parents listed. Source – TD

SAUVAGES
Francois, a Montagnais Indian, appartenant a Jacques De la Fontaine, born 1737, baptized 14 Dec. 1747 at Quebec. No marriage listed. Source – TD

SAUVAGES
Francois, a Micmac, born July 1703, baptized 4 Sept. 1703 at Ste-Anne, Quebec. No parents or marriage listed.
Source – TD

SAUVAGES
Francois, a Amalecite of Acadie, baptized 13 June 1749 at Quebec. No marriage listed. Source – TD

SAUVAGES
Francois, an Algonquin, baptized 16 Jan. 1714 at St-Francois, I. J. No parents listed. Source – TD

SAUVAGES
Francois, an Abenaquis, baptized 9 June 1746 at Quebec. No marriage listed. Source – TD

SAUVAGES (GORGENDIERE?)
Francois-Michel, adopted by messier Joseph De la Gorgendiere, baptized 11 Aug. 1758 at Ste-Foye, Quebec. No marriage listed. Source – TD

SAUVAGES
Francois-Denis, a Creole, born 1727, baptized 31 March 1739 at Quebec. No marriage listed. Source – TD

SAUVAGES
Francois Normand of Ouaspoux, a Metis, died 18 June 1750 at Quebec (Il avait faitfait ses paques ice). No marriage listed. Sourc e – TD

SAUVAGES
Francois-Xavier, baptized 1760, died 5 Feb. 1774 at St-Joseph, Beauce, Quebec. No parents listed. Source – TD

SAUVAGES
Francois-Xavier, an Abenaquis, born 1726, died 12 Sept. 1746 at Quebec. No marriage listed. Source – TD

SAUVAGES
Francoise, baptized 7 Jan. 1705 at Montreal, Quebec. No parents listed. Source – TD

SAUVAGES
Francoise, appartenant a M. de Beaurivage, born 1731, died 15 August 1747 at Quebec. Source – TD

SAUVAGES
Francoise, baptized 1673, died 24 March 1713 at St-Pierre, Quebec. Source – TD

SAUVAGES

Francoise Sauvages, an Abenaquise, baptism 11 Dec. 1709 at Quebec. No marriage listed. Source – TD

SAUVAGES

Francoise, an Algonquine, baptized 16 Oct. 1713 at Trois-Rivieres, Quebec. Source – TD

SAUVAGES

Francoise-Angelique, an Abenaquise, baptized 11 Oct. 1772 at St-Joseph, Beauce, Quebec. No parents listed. Source – TD

SAUVAGES

Francoise-Louise Sauvages, baptism 6 Jan. 1707 at Quebec. No marriage listed. Source – TD

SAUVAGES

Francoise-Ursule, baptized 1 Nov. 1734 at la Baie-du Febvre, Quebec. Source – TD

SAUVAGES

Gabriel Sauvages, an Amalecite, baptism 1703, death 9 Aug. 1709 at Quebec. Source – TD

SAUVAGES

Genevieve, baptized Nov. and died 1 Dec. 1757 at Riviere-Ouelle, Quebec. No parents listed. Source – TD

SAUVAGES

Genevieve, appartenant of Mne. Besancon, born 1734, baptized 18 May 1760, died 10 June 1760 at Beauport, Quebec. No marriage listed. Source – TD

SAUVAGES

Gregoire, an Amalecite, baptized 21 July 1734 at Kamourask, Quebec. No parents listed. Source – TD

SAUVAGES
Gregoire, born and died 24 Feb. 1717 at Ste-Anne-de-la-Pocatiere, Quebec. No parents listed. Source – TD

SAUVAGES
Gregoire of Pictou, Acadie, baptized 5 May 1746 at Quebec. No marriage listed. Source – TD

SAUVAGES
Helene, born 1742 at Acadie, baptized 21 June 1744 at Quebec. No marriage listed. Source – TD

SAUVAGES
Honore, appartenant a M. Olivier D'Heman, medecin de la Martinique, born 1722, baptized 6 Sept. 1739 at Quebec. No marriage listed. Source – TD

SAUVAGES
Hypolite, a Panis Indian, appartenant of M. Fleury de la Gorgendiere, born 1718, baptized 7 Jan. 1733, died 26 Jan. 1733 at Ste-Anne-de-la-Perade, Quebec. No parents listed. Source – TD

SAUVAGES
Ignace, a Micmac, born 26 Aug. 1704, baptized 27 Aug. 1704 at Ste-Anne, Quebec. No parents or marriage listed. Source – TD

SAUVAGES
Jacques Sauvages, an Abenaquis, baptism 1665, died 12 May 1710 at Quebec. No marriage listed. Source – TD

SAUVAGES
Jaqueline Sauvages, an Abenaquise, baptism 1690, died 27 Feb. 1702 at Quebec. Source – TD

SAUVAGES
Jacques-Alexis Sauvages, an Abenaquis, baptism 26 Aug.
1709 at Quebec. No marriage listed. Source – TD

SAUVAGES
Jacques Sauvages, baptism 11 Nov. 1707 at Quebec. No
marriage listed. Source – TD

SAUVAGES
Jacques, an Abenaquis, born 1733, died 22 June 1746 at
Quebec. Source – TD

SAUVAGES
Jacques, an Iroquois of Sault-St-Louis, baptized 1754, died 1
March 1770 at St-Joseph, Beauce, Quebec. No parents listed.
Source – TD

SAUVAGES
Jacques, appartenant of M. De la Perade, born 1737, died 4
July 1742 at Ste-Anne-de-la-Perade, Quebec. No parents
listed. Source – TD

SAUVAGES
Jacques Sauvages, baptism 6 April 1694 at Quebec. No
marriage listed. Source – TD

SAUVAGES
Jacques-Charles, a Montagnais, born 1730, baptized 26 Jan.
1738 at Quebec. Died 7 Sept. 1740. Source – TD

SAUVAGES
Jacques-Etienne of Becancour, baptized 28 Aug. 1768 at St-
Joseph, Beauce, Quebec. No parents listed. Source – TD

SAUVAGES
Jacques-Nicolas, appartenant a M. Breard, born 1745, baptized 30 March 1753 at Quebec. No marriage listed. Source – TD

SAUVAGES
Jean, an Abenaquis, of St-Francois, baptized 1 Oct. 1769 at St-Joseph, Beauce, Quebec. No parents listed. Source – TD

SAUVAGES
Jean, baptized 1712, died 28 March 1717 at Ste-Anne-de-la-Pocatiere, Quebec. No parents listed. Source – TD

SAUVAGES
Jean, an Abenaquis, baptized 25 Aug. 1771 at St-Joseph, Beauce, Quebec. No parents listed. Source – TD

SAUVAGES
Jean, an Algonquin married Charlotte ....?, veuve de Guillaume of Chicoutimi on 25 Feb. 1779 at Ste-Anne-de-la-Perade, Quebec. Source – TD

SAUVAGES
Jean, appartenant a M. Page, born 1729, baptized and died 9 Nov. 1741 at Quebec. Source – TD

SAUVAGES
Jean-Amable of I'lle-Royale, baptized 25 April 1746 at Quebec. No marriage listed. Source – TD

SAUVAGES
Jean-Baptiste-Augustin-Xavier Sauvages, an Abenaquis, baptism 23 March 1758 at Quebec. Source – TD

SAUVAGES
Jean-Baptiste, a Montagnais Indian, appartenant a Pierre Emond, born 1739, baptized 24 Sept. 1743 at Quebec. No marriage listed. Source – TD

SAUVAGES
Jean-Baptiste, baptized 1721, died 31 Dec. 1723 at St-Pierre, Quebec. Parents not listed. Source – TD

SAUVAGES
Jean-Baptiste, appartenant a Pierre Emond, born 1737, died 10 Sept. 1744 at Quebec. Source – TD

SAUVAGES
Jean-Baptiste, an Outaouis, born 1735, baptized 6 Jan. 1750 at Quebec. No marriage listed. Source – TD

SAUVAGES
Jean-Baptiste Sauvages, an Etchemin, baptism 29 July 1692 at Quebec. Record says born 1620 but probably is 1690? No marriage record. Source – TD

SAUVAGES
Jean-Baptiste Sauvages, a Panis, baptism 5 August 1700 at Quebec. No marriage listed. Source – TD

SAUVAGES
Jean-Baptiste Sauvages of Pantagouet, born March 1704, baptism 10 June 1704 at Quebec. No marriage listed.
 Source – TD

SAUVAGES
Jean-Baptiste Sauvages, a Micmac, baptism 24 Aug. 1713 at Quebec. No marriage listed. Source – TD

SAUVAGES
Jean-Baptiste, a Huron, baptized 23 Aug. 1704 at Pte-aux-Trembles, Quebec. No marriage listed. Source – TD

SAUVAGES
Jean-Baptiste, baptized 17 Sept. 1756 at Riviere-Ouelle, Quebec. No parents listed. Source – TD

SAUVAGES
Jean-Baptiste, a Micmac, born 1702, baptized 13 July 1703 at Ste-Anne, Quebec. No parents or marriage listed.
Source – TD

SAUVAGES
Jean-Baptiste, a Micmac, baptized 1754, died 8 Nov. 1755 at St-Augustin< Quebec. No parents listed. Source – TD

SAUVAGES
Jean-Baptiste, an Abenaquis, baptisted 3 Nov. 1760 at St-Joseph, Beauce, Quebec. No parents listed. Source – TD

SAUVAGES
Jean-Baptiste Sauvage, an Abenaquis, baptism 30 Aug. 1727 at Quebec. Source – TD

SAUVAGES
Jean-Baptiste Sauvages, a Panis, appartenant a Jean Mariette, born 1711, baptism 10 Nov. 1719 at Quebec. Source – TD

SAUVAGES
Jean-Baptiste Sauvages, a Tamarois, born 1693, baptism 21 June 1701 at Quebec. No marriage listed. Source – TD

SAUVAGES
Jean-Charles, a Micmac, baptized 9 Dec. 1738 at Kamouraska, Quebec. No parents listed. Source – TD

SAUVAGES
Jean-Francois, baptized 1 July 1770 at St-Joseph, Beauce, Quebec. No parents listed. Source – TD

SAUVAGES
Jean-Louis, a Minmac, baptized 11 June 1748 at Quebec. No marriage listed. Source – TD

SAUVAGES
Jean-Marie, an Abenaquis of St-Francois, baptized 24 Feb. 1771 at St-Joseph, Beauce, Quebec. No parents listed. Source – TD

SAUVAGES
Jean-Marie-Nicolas, Sauvages, born 1723, baptized 13 March 1738 at Lorette, Quebec. No marriage listed. Source – TD

SAUVAGES
Jean-Taxous, chief of the Abenaquis died 12 Feb. 1720 at Quebec. Source – TD

SAUVAGES
Jean-Thomas Sauvages, baptism 1640, death 9 April 1710 at Quebec. No marriage listed. Source – TD

SAUVAGES
Jeanne-Francoise-Cudule, appartenant of M. Galineau, seigneur of Ste-Marie, Quebec, born 1701, baptized 9 Jan. 1741 at Ste-Anne-de-la-Perade, Quebec. No marriage listed. Source – TD

SAUVAGES
Jeanne, an Abenaquise, baptized 4 Sept. 1713 at Trois-Rivieres, Quebec. Source – TD

SAUVAGES
Joseph, a Panis, born 1730, baptized 19 March 1744 at St-Pierre, Quebec. No marriage listed. Source – TD

SAUVAGES
Joseph, appartenant of M. Gautier, a Tanner, born 1725, baptized 21 Dec. 1739 at Ste-Anne-de-la-Perade, Quebec. No marriage listed. Source – TD

SAUVAGES
Joseph, an Abenaquis, baptized 24 July 1746 at Quebec. No marriage listed. Source – TD

SAUVAGES
Joseph, an Abenaquis, baptized 1730, died 20 Dec. 1760 at St-Joseph, Beauce, Quebec. No marriage or parents listed.
Source – TD

SAUVAGES
Joseph, a Micmac, born 29 June 1703, baptized 13 July 1703 at Ste-Anne, Quebec. No parents or marriage listed.
Source – TD

SAUVAGES
Joseph, a Micmac, baptized 12 Dec. 1712 at Ste-Anne, Quebec. No marriage or parents listed. Source – TD

SAUVAGES
Joseph, baptized 1735, died 4 Aug. 1749 at Riviere-Ouelle, Quebec. No parents listed. Source – TD

SAUVAGES
Joseph et Marie Sauvages, a Micmac, baptism 14 Aug. 1748 at Quebec. No marriage listed. Source – TD

SAUVAGES
Joseph-Adrien, appartenant of Pierre-Francois DeVaudreuil, governor; filleul d'Adrien Gourdeau, born 1751, baptized 18 Oct. 1757 at Trois-Rivieres, Quebec. Source – TD

SAUVAGES
Joseph-Gabriel, a Patocas Indian, appartenant a M. De la Tesserie, born 1727, baptized 20 Oct. 1737 at Quebec. No marriage listed. Source – TD

SAUVAGES
Joseph-Laurent, baptized 7 Jan. 1717 at Ste-Anne-de-la-Pocatiere, Quebec. No parents listed. Source – TD

SAUVAGES
Joseph-Nicolas Sauvages of Missouri, adopte par Joseph Legris, born 1722, baptism 18 July 1731 at Quebec. Source – TD

SAUVAGES
Joseph-Thomas Sauvages, an Abenaquis, born Feb. 1705, baptism 23 April 1705 at Quebec. No marriage listed. Source – TD

SAUVAGES
Joseph Sauvages, a Micmac, born 1734, died 26 Aug. 1769 at Quebec. Source – TD

SAUVAGES
Joseph, born 1717, baptized c. 1717, died 25 Aug. 1757 at General Hospital, M. (Montreal?), Quebec. No parents or wife listed. Source – TD

SAUVAGES
Joseph Sauvages, an Abenaquis, baptism 26 Aug. 1709 at Quebec. No marriage listed. Source – TD

SAUVAGES
Joseph Sauvages, a Micmac, baptism 6 Sept. 1697 at Quebec.
No marriage listed. Source – TD

SAUVAGES
Joseph-Francois Sauvages, born 1728, baptized 17 June 1736
at Quebec. No marriage listed. Source – TD

SAUVAGES
Joseph-Louis, an Abenaquis of Acadie, born and died 2 Aug.
1772 at St-Joseph, Beauce, Quebec. No parents listed.
Source – TD

SAUVAGES
Joseph-Marie, baptized 1731, died 8 Jan. 1761 at St-Joseph,
Beauce, Quebec. No parents or marriage listed. Source – TD

SAUVAGES
LaRose, eleve chez M. Montendre, born ? Died 5 Oct. 1760 at
Ste-Anne-de-la-Perade, Quebec. No parents listed.
Source – TD

SAUVAGES
Louis, appartenant a Louis Volant d'Haubourg, born 1734,
baptized 12 May 1753 at Quebec. No marriage listed.
Source – TD

SAUVAGES
Louis, a Panis Indian, appartenant of Claude Gouin, born
1731, baptized 15 Sept. 1735 at Ste-Anne-de-la-Perade,
Quebec. No marriage listed. Source – TD

SAUVAGES
Louis, baptized 4 April 1760, aux Eboulements. No parents or
marriage listed. Source – TD

SAUVAGES
Louis, born 1692, baptized 13 Aug. 1702 at Ste-Anne, Quebec. No parents or marriage listed. Source – TD

SAUVAGES
Louis, an Iroquois of Lac-des-Deux-Montagnes, baptized 1772, died 6 Feb. 1773 at St-Joseph, Beauce, Quebec. No parents listed. Source – TD

SAUVAGES
Louis, an Abenaquis, baptized 31 Oct. 1760 at St-Joseph, Beauce, Quebec. No parents listed. Source – TD

SAUVAGES
Louis, born 1730, died 24 Aug. 1744 at Quebec. Source – TD

SAUVAGES
Louis, an Iroquois of Lac-des-Deux-Montagnes, baptized 16 Feb. 1772 at St-Joseph, Beauce, Quebec. No parents listed. Source – TD

SAUVAGES
Louis Sauvages, born 1750, died 22 Feb. 1752 at Quebec. Source – TD

SAUVAGES
Louis Sauvages, baptism 7 Feb. 1706 at Quebec. No marriage listed. Source – TD

SAUVAGES
Louis-Francois, a Montagnais, appartenant a Francois Volant, born 1744, baptized 12 May 1753 at Quebec. No marriages listed. Source – TD

SAUVAGES
Louis-Jacques, appartenant a Louis Parant, baptized 29 Oct.
1752 at Quebec. No marriage listed. Source – TD

SAUVAGES
Louis-Joseph, a Panis, appartenant a M. Monier, born 1739,
baptized 14 Aug. 1753 at Quebec. No marriage listed.
Source – TD

SAUVAGES
Louis-Joseph et Louise-Marie, born 1737, baptized 22 July
1744 at Quebec. No marriage listed. Source – TD

SAUVAGES
Louis-Joseph-Isidore of Cordule, appartenant of M. Gatineau,
baptized 12 March 1737 at Ste-Anne-de-la-Perade, Quebec.
No marriage listed. Source – TD

SAUVAGES
Louis-Philippe, appartenant a M. Philippe Denis, baptized 3
June 1746 at Quebec. No marriage listed. Source – TD

SAUVAGES
Louis-Thomas, a Patocas, appartenant a M. Francois Cugnet,
born 1741, baptized 25 March 1751 at Quebec. No marriage
listed. Source – TD

SAUVAGES
Louise, baptized 20 April 1718 at St-Pierre, Quebec and died
the same day. Parents not listed. Source – TD

SAUVAGES
Louise, appartenant of M. Louis Gouin, baptized 1745, died
31 Dec. 1760 at Ste-Anne-de-la-Perade, Quebec. No parents
listed. Source – TD

SAUVAGES
Louise-Angelique, appartenant a Mm. De la Ronde, born 1726, baptized 5 Oct. 1741 at Quebec. No marriage listed. Source –TD

SAUVAGES
Louise, a Montagnaise Indian, born 1711, baptized 28 May 1741 at Quebec. No marriage listed. Source – TD

SAUVAGES
Louise Sauvages, baptism 1682, death 11 Feb. 1712 at Quebec. Source – TD

SAUVAGES
Louise, a Panise Indian, appartenant at M. De la Perade, born 1723, baptized 24 Feb. 1731 at Ste-Anne-de-la-Perade, Quebec, died 9 May 1742. No marriage listed. Source – TD

SAUVAGES
Louise, a Montagnaise, born 1732, died 25 July 1742 at Quebec. Source – TD

SAUVAGES
Louise-Agnes, an Abenaquise, baptized 20 Aug. 1746 at Quebec. No marriage listed. Source – TD

SAUVAGES
Louise-Catherine, a Huron, baptized 24 Aug. 1704 at Pte-aux-Trembles, Quebec. No marriage listed. Source – TD

SAUVAGES
Louise-Francoise Sauvages, baptism 24 June 1693 at Quebec. No marriage listed. Source – TD

SAUVAGES
Louise-Ignace-Suzanne, appartenant of M. Gatineau, born
1724, baptized 9 Jan. 1741 at Ste-Anne-de-la-Perade, Quebec.
No marriage listed. Source – TD

SAUVAGES
Luc, a Micmac, born 1744, died 10 August 1747 at Quebec.
Source – TD

SAUVAGES
Luc-Moution, Died 19 Nov. 1718 at St-Pierre, Quebec. No
parents listed. Source – TD

SAUVAGES
Madeleine, a Micmac, born 1687, died 26 August 1747 at
Quebec. No marriage listed. Source – TD

SAUVAGES
Madeleine, born 1742, died 22 Jan 1758 at Quebec.
Source – TD

SAUVAGES
Madeleine, an Abenaquise of Acadie, born 1767, baptized 15
June 1772 at St-Joseph, Beauce, Quebec. (Soeur du
precedent). No parents listed. Source – TD

SAUVAGES
Madeleine, born and died 3 April 1717 at Ste-Anne-de-la-
Pocatiere, Quebec. No parents listed. Source – TD

SAUVAGES
Madeleine of Labrador, appartenant a M. Charles L'Arche,
born 1731, died 6 March 1741 at Quebec. Source – TD

SAUVAGES
Madeleine-Marie-Anne, appartenant of M. De la Perade, born
1732, baptized 12 June 1743 at Ste-Anne-de-la-Perade,
Quebec. No marriage listed. Source – TD

SAUVAGES
Marguerite (Onodoca), baptized 2 Feb. 1713 at Chambly.
(Baptized dans le bois par Pierre Pepin-Laforce). No parents
listed. Source – TD

SAUVAGES
Marguerite, a Montagnaise, died 15 May 1715 at Ste-Anne,
Quebec. No parents listed. Source – TD

SAUVAGES
Marguerite, du Mistassin, born 1762, baptized 23 Sept. 1766
at la Baie-St-Paul, Quebec. No parents or marriage listed.
Source – TD

SAUVAGES
Marguerite, an Abenaquise was baptized 27 July 1732 at
Quebec. Source – TD

SAUVAGES
Marguerite Sauvages, appartenant a M. Chasle, baptism 1707,
death 14 Nov. 1719 at Quebec. Source – TD

SAUVAGES
Marguerite, an Algonquine, baptized 8 Oct. 1713 at Trois-
Riviere, Quebec. Source – TD

SAUVAGES
Marguerite du Labrador, appartenant a M. De Beaurivage,
born 1708, died 27 March 1743 at Quebec. No marriage listed.
Source – TD

SAUVAGES
Marguerite-Catherine, appartenant a M. De Berman, born
1728, baptized 28 Aug. 1741 at Quebec. No marriage listed.
Source – TD

SAUVAGES
Marguerite, a Amalecite, baptized 27 Dec. 1731 at
Kamouraska, Quebec. No parents listed. Source – TD

SAUVAGES
Marguerite, a Montagnaise, appartenant a veuve Cote, born
1720, baptized 4 Sept. 1745 at Quebec. No marriage listed.
Source – TD

SAUVAGES
Marguerite Sauvages, born 1717, baptism 16 July 1718 at
Quebec. No marriage listed. Source – TD

SAUVAGES
Marguerite-Francoise Sauvages, a Panise, born 1704, baptism
17 April 1718 at Quebec. No marriage listed. Source – TD

SAUVAGES
Marie, born 1729, died 18 Oct. 1748 at Quebec. Source – TD

SAUVAGES
Marie, femme d'Etienne Aneschom, died 9 Aug. 1707 at Ste-
Anne, Quebec. Source – TD

SAUVAGES
Marie, an Iroquoise of Lac-des-Deux-Montagnes, baptized 6
Feb. 1773 at St-Joseph, Beauce, Quebec. No parents listed.
Source – TD

SAUVAGES
Marie, an Abenaquise, baptized 1753, died 24 Dec. 1760 at St-Joseph, Beauce, Quebec. No parents listed. Source – TD

SAUVAGES
Marie, a Micmac, born 1730, died 10 Nov. 1748 at Quebec. Source – TD

SAUVAGES
Marie, an Abenaquise, born 1697, died 10 Nov. 1747 at Quebec. No marriage listed. Source – TD

SAUVAGES
Marie, baptized 1728, died 11 Oct. 1733 at St-Augustin, Quebec, daughter of the precedente. Source – TD

SAUVAGES
Marie, an Abenaquise, baptized 1759, died 17 Dec. 1760 at St-Joseph, Beauce, Quebec. No parents listed. Source – TD

SAUVAGES
Marie, born 1708, baptized 24 Dec. 1748 at Quebec. No marriage listed. Source – TD

SAUVAGES
Marie, an Illinoise Indian born 1701, died 17 Dec. 1729 at Quebec. No marriage listed. Source – TD

SAUVAGES
Marie-Agathe, an Abenaquise, baptized 14 Aug. 1738 at Quebec. No marriage listed. Source – TD

SAUVAGES
Marie-Anne, baptized 1680, died 8 Sept. 1736 at Terrebonne. No parents listed. Source – TD

SAUVAGES
Marie-Anne, a Micmac, baptized 11 Feb. 1739 at
Kamouraska, Quebec. No parents listed. Source – TD

SAUVAGES
Marie-Anne, a Micmac, born 1699, baptized 26 July 1701 at
Ste-Anne, Quebec. No parents or husband listed. Source – TD

SAUVAGES
Marie-Anne, baptized 17 Oct. 1749 at Riviere-Ouelle, Quebec.
No parents listed. Source – TD

SAUVAGES
Marie-Anne, a Montagnaise, baptized 10 July 1715 at Ste-
Anne, Quebec. No parents or husband listed. Source – TD

SAUVAGES
Marie-Anne, baptized 16 Sept. 1746 at Quebec. No marriage
listed. Source – TD

SAUVAGES
Marie-Anne, baptized 1 Aug. 1719 at Lachine. No parents
listed. Source – TD

SAUVAGES
Marie-Anne Sauvages, a Panise, appartenant a M. Claude
Legris, born 1712, baptism 26 Jan. 1721 at Quebec.
Source – TD

SAUVAGES
Marie-Anne, appartenant a Louise DeFleury, born 1731,
baptized 21 Sept. 1736 at Quebec. No marriage listed.
Source – TD

SAUVAGES
Marie-Anne, appartenant a M. de Beaujeu-Villemonde, born 1740, baprized 14 Jan. 1755 at Quebec. No marriage listed. Source – TD

SAUVAGES
Marie-Anne, born 1740, baptized 17 May 1755 at Longueuil. (Domestic of Francois-Pierre Cherrier, medecin). No parents listed. Source – TD

SAUVAGES
Marie-Anne, a Montagnaise, appartenant a M. De Fleury, born 1731, died 27 April 1742 at Quebec. Source – TD

SAUVAGES
Marie-Anne Sauvages, an Abenaquise, baptism 1707, death 15 April 1715 at Quebec. Source – TD

SAUVAGES
Marie-Anne-Joseph, appartenant of M. De la Perade, born 1704, baptized 2 Feb. 1735 at Ste-Anne-de-la-Perade, Quebec, died 5 May 1740. No marriage listed. Source – TD

SAUVAGES
Marie-Apolline Sauvages, an Abenaquise, baptism 1702, death 26 July 1710 at Quebec. Source – TD

SAUVAGES
Marie-Anne Sauvages, a Panise, appartenant a M. Ambroise Renoyer, born 1707, baptism 24 June 1719 at Quebec. Source – TD

SAUVAGES
Marie-Anne Sauvages, born Sept. 1724 at Acadie and baptism 1 Oct. 1724 at Quebec. Source – TD

SAUVAGES
Marie-Anne, a Micmac, born 25 July 1706, baptized 26 July 1706 at Ste-Anne, Quebec. No parents or marriage listed. Source – TD

SAUVAGES
Marie-Anne, appartenant of M. De la Perade, born 1717, baptized 9 April 1742 at Ste-Anne-de-la-Perade, Quebec. No marriage listed. Source – TD

SAUVAGES
Marie-Anne Sauvages, born 1696, died 24 Sept. 1758 at Quebec. No marriage listed. Source – TD

SAUVAGES
Marie Sauvages, an Abenaquise, born Nov. 1715, baptism 30 July 1716 at Quebec. No marriage listed. Source – TD

SAUVAGES
Marie-Catherine, appartenant a M. Breard, born 1743, baptized 30 March 1753 at Quebec. No marriage listed. Source – TD

SAUVAGES
Marie-DE-Sebastien, an Abenaquise, born Feb. 1736, died 1 March 1736 at Quebec. Source – TD

SAUVAGES
Marie-Genevieve, baptized 16 Oct. 1769 at St-Joseph, Beauce, Quebec. No parents listed. Source – TD

SAUVAGES
Marie-Jeanne, baptized 24 June 1720 at Lachine. No parents listed. Source – TD

SAUVAGES
Marie-Jeanne, a Malicite Indian, baptized 20 May 1737 at
Quebec. No marriage listed. Source – TD

SAUVAGES
Marie-Jeanne, a Montagnaise, appartenant a Francois Simon,
born 1732, baptized 17 April 1746 at Quebec. No marriage
listed. Source – TD

SAUVAGES
Marie-Jeanne, born 1745, died 15 Nov. 1748 at Quebec.
Source – TD

SAUVAGES
Marie Sauvages, baptism 23 April 1712 at Quebec. No
marriage listed. Source – TD

SAUVAGES
Marie Sauvages, appartenant a veuve Duplessis, born 1702,
baptism 20 Aug. 1723 at Quebec. Source – TD

SAUVAGES
Marie, an Abenaquise of Becancour, baptized 26 May 1755 at
St-Joseph, Beauce, Quebec. No parents or marriage listed.
Source – TD

SAUVAGES
Marie Sauvages, a Panise, appartenant a M. DeLouvigny, born
1704, baptism 29 May 1718 at Quebec. Source – TD

SAUVAGES
Marie, a Micmac, born 1730, died 10 Nov. 1748 at Quebec.
Source – TD

SAUVAGES
Marie, born 1719, died 2 Feb. 1749 at Quebec. Source – TD

SAUVAGES
Marie of Acadie, baptized 10 Oct. 1773 at St-Joseph, Beauce,
Quebec. No parents listed. Source – TD

SAUVAGES
Marie, appartenant of M. De la Perade, baptized 1725, died 12
April 1738 at Ste-Anne-de-la-Perade, Quebec. No parents
listed. Source – TD

SAUVAGES
Marie, appartenant a M. De Beaurivage, born 1730, died 24
April 1738 at Quebec. Source – TD

SAUVAGES
Marie of l'Acadie, born 1764, baptized 4 Jan. 1767 at St-
Joseph, Beauce, Quebec. No parents listed. Source – TD

SAUVAGES
Marie, born 1744, died 18 August 1746 at Quebec.
Source – TD

SAUVAGES
Marie, baptized 1743, died 3 Dec. 1745 at St-Joseph, Beauce,
Quebec. No parents listed. Source – TD

SAUVAGES
Marie, baptized 1 April 1698 at la Baie-St-Paul, Quebec. No
parents or marriage listed. Source – TD

SAUVAGES
Marie, a Micmac, baptized 1773, died 23 May 1787 at l'Ile-
Verte. No parents listed. Source – TD

SAUVAGES
Marie, born 1733, died 5 March 1745 at Quebec. Source – TD

SAUVAGES
Marie Sauvages, an Abenaquise, baptism 18 Dec. 1722 at Quebec. No marriage listed. Source – TD

SAUVAGES
Marie-Eulalie, an Abenquise, born 1741, died 20 Oct. 1744 at Quebec. Source – TD

SAUVAGES
Marie-Francoise, an Abenaquise of St-Francois, baptized 1 Oct. 1769 at St-Joseph, Beauce, Quebec. No parents listed. Source – TD

SAUVAGES
Marie-Francoise, an Abenaquise, baptized 18 Jan. 1767 at St-Joseph, Beauce, Quebec. No parents listed. Source – TD

SAUVAGES
Marie-Francoise Sauvages, baptism 24 June 1693 at Quebec. No marriages listed. Source – TD

SAUVAGES
Marie-Francoise et Marguerite, a Micmac, baptized 17 July 1716 at Ste-Anne, Quebec. No parents or husband listed. Source – TD

SAUVAGES
Marie-Francoise, died 23 Feb. 1760, aux Eboulements. No parents or marriage listed. Source – TD

SAUVAGES
Marie-Francoise Sauvages, an Abenaquise, baptism 7 July 1708 at Quebec. No marriage listed. Source – TD

SAUVAGES
Marie-Francoise, baptized 29 July 1714 at Trois-Riviere,
Quebec. Source – TD

SAUVAGES
Marie-Francoise Sauvages, a Panise, appartenant a Mnn
Cheron, born 1714, baptism 10 July 1724 at Quebec.
Source – TD

SAUVAGES
Marrie-Francoise Sauvages, an Arkansas, born 1712, baptism
26 Feb. 1719 at Quebec. No marriage listed. Source – TD

SAUVAGES
Marie-Jeanne Sauvages, an Abenaquise, born May 1705,
baptism 1 June 1705 at Quebec. No marriage listed.
Source – TD

SAUVAGES
Marie-Catherine, an Algonquinne, baptized 21 April 1738 at
Ste-Genevieve. No marriage listed. Source – TD

SAUVAGES
Marie-Catherine Sauvages, an Anapol, baptism 17 Feb. 1706
at Quebec. No marriage listed. Source – TD

SAUVAGES
Marie-Edmee, baptized 1706, died 18 Nov. 1707 at Ste-Anne,
Quebec. No parents listed. Source – TD

SAUVAGES
Marie-Genevieve, a Micmac, baptized 12 aug. 1733 at
Kamouraska, Quebec. No parents listed. Source – TD

SAUVAGES
Maire-Genevieve, a Montagnaise, baptized 3 March 1730 at
Kamouraska, Quebec. No parents listed. Source – TD

SAUVAGES
Marie-Joseph, Micmac, born 5 Aug. 1707, baptized 15 Aug.
1707 at Ste-Anne, Quebec. No parents or marriage listed.
Source – TD

SAUVAGES
Marie-Joseph, appartenant au Sieur Charles Alavoine,
chevalier, born around 1772, dans l'ouest, baptized 4 April
1783 at St-Cuthbert, Quebec. Source – TD

SAUVAGES
Marie-Joseph, a Patocas, born 1726, baptized 6 DEC. 1733 aT
Ste-Genevieve, Quebec. No marriage listed. Source – TD

SAUVAGES
Marie-Joseph, appartenant of M. Chalou, born 1730, baptized
18 May 1760 at Beauport, Quebec. No marriage listed.
Source – TD

SAUVAGES
Marie-Joseph, baptized 1 Sept. 1747 at Quebec. No marriage
listed. Source – TD

SAUVAGES
Marie-Joseph of the nation of Brochets, vers la mer de l'ouest,
born 1728, baptized 30 June 1743 at Quebec. No marriage
listed. Source – TD

SAUVAGES
Marie-Joseph, an Algonquine Indian, baptized 21 Dec. 1740 at
Quebec. No marriage listed. Source – TD

SAUVAGES
Marie-Joseph, a Panise Indian, born 1730, baptized 1 April 1741 at Quebec. Source – TD

SAUVAGES
Marie-Joseph, appartenant of M. De la Perade, born 1719, died 3 April 1742 at Ste-Anne-de-la-Perade, Quebec. No marriage listed. Source – TD

SAUVAGES
Marie-Joseph, born 1748, baptized 27 July 1768 a Lachenaye. No parents or husband listed. Source – TD

SAUVAGES
Marie-Joseph, Siouse, appartenant a Antoine Gautier, born 1738, baptized 7 March 1745 at Quebec. No marriage listed. Source – TD

SAUVAGES
Marie-Joseph of the nation of Crochets, appartenant a M. Riverin, born 1738, baptized 15 Aug. 1750 at Quebec. No marriage listed. Source – TD

SAUVAGES
Marie-Joseph, appartenant a Damours-Deplaine, born 1740, baptized 5 June 1752 at Quebec. No marriage listed. Source – TD

SAUVAGES
Marie-Joseph Sauvages, appartenant a veuve Cadet, born 1708, baptism 11 Jan. 1722 at Quebec. Source – TD

SAUVAGES
Marie-Joseph, an Abenaquise of Becancour, baptized 14 March 1762 at St-Joseph, Beauce, Quebec. No parents listed. Source – TD

SAUVAGES
Marie-Joseph Sauvages, a Huronne, baptism 4 May 1693 at
Quebec. No marriage listed. Source – TD

SAUVAGES
Marie-Judith, an Amalecite, baptized 5 April 1733 at
Kamouraska, Quebec. No parents listed. Source – TD

SAUVAGES
Marie-Louise, an Algonquinne, baptized 29 Jan. 1739 at Ste-
Genevieve, Quebec. No marriage listed. Source – TD

SAUVAGES
Marie-Louise of Franchon, appartenant of M. De la Perade,
Quebec baptized 11 Oct. 1741 at Ste-Anne-de-la-Perade,
Quebec. No marriage listed. Source – TD

SAUVAGES
Marie-Louise, born 1737, baptized 3 May 1749 at Quebec. No
marriage listed. Source – TD

SAUVAGES
Marie-Louise, appartenant a Julien Joly, born 1740, baptized
11 Oct. 1743 at Quebec. No marriage listed. Source – TD

SAUVAGES
Marie-Louise, a Montagnaise, appartenant a Dme veuve
Fornel, born 1747, died 5 Dec. 1748 at Quebec. Source – TD

SAUVAGES
Marie-Louise Sauvages, of Acadie, baptism 20 Oct. 1697 at
Quebec. No marriage listed. Source – TD

SAUVAGES
Marie-Louise Sauvages, a Micmac, baptism 16 June 1697 at
Quebec. No marriage listed. Source – TD

SAUVAGES
Marie-Louise, baptized 17 Nov. 1776 at St-Joseph, Beauce,
Quebec. No parents listed. Source – TD

SAVUAGES
Marie-Louise, appartenant a Julien Joly, born 1740, died 22
July 1746 at Quebec. Source – TD

SAUVAGES
Marie-Louise of St. Domingue, achetee la par M. Lachenaye,
born 1717, baptized 30 August 1732 at Quebec. No marriage
listed. Source – TD

SAUVAGES
Marie-Louise, a Papinochoise, born 1730, baptized 12 Nov.
1732 at Quebec. Source – TD

SAUVAGES
Marie-Louise of Acadie, baptized 8 Dec. 1771 at St-Joseph,
Beauce, Quebec. No parents listed. Source – TD

SAUVAGES
Marie-Louise, appartenant a veuve Langlois, born 1716, died
1733 at Quebec. No marriage listed. Source – TD

SAUVAGES
Marie-Louise-Genevieve Sauvages, appartenant a Mnn
Chambalon, baptism 1706, death 25 April 1719 at Quebec.
Source – TD

SAUVAGES
Marie-Louise-Jacqueline, appartenant of M. Gatineau, born
1732, baptized 26 Dec. 1737 at Ste-Anne-de-la-Perade,
Quebec. No marriage listed. Source – TD

SAUVAGES
Marie-Madeleine, an Amalecite, baptized 30 Dec. 1731 at
Kamouraska, Quebec. No parents listed. Source – TD

SAUVAGES
Marie-Madeleine, born May 1702, baptized 13 Aug. 1702 at
Ste-Anne, Quebec. No parents or marriage listed.
Source – TD

SAUVAGES
Marie-Madeleine, a Micmac, baptized 1725, died 19 May
1729 at Kamouraska, Quebec. No parents listed. Source – TD

SAUVAGES
Marie-Madeleine, baptized 28 Aug. 1768 at St-Joseph,
Beauce, Quebec, died 1 April 1770. No parents listed.
Source – TD

SAUVAGES
Marie-Madeleine, baptized 24 Nov. 1729 at Pte-aux-Trembles,
Quebec. No marriage listed. Source – TD

SAUVAGES
Marie-Madeleine, baptized 30 Sept. 1726 at Pte-aux-
Trembles, Quebec. No marriage listed. Source – TD

SAUVAGES
Marie-Madeleine, an Algonquine, baptized 8 Sept. 1713 at aux
Trois-Rivieres, Quebec. Source – TD

SAUVAGES
Marie-Madeleine, appartenant of Pierre Rivard-Lanouette,
born 1727, baptized 10 April 1742 at Ste-de-la-Perade,
Quebec. No marriage listed. Source – TD

SAUVAGES
Marie-Madeleine, of Becancour, baptized 1 Aug. 1751 at
Quebec. No marriage listed. Source – TD

SAUVAGES
Marie-Madeleine, a Micmac from Miramichi, (New
Brunswick) baptized 30 July 1741 at Quebec. No marriage
listed. Source – TD

SAUVAGES
Marie-Madeleine Sauvages, a Tete-platte, appartenant a M.
Martin Curot, born 1717, baptism 17 July 1723 at Quebec.
Source – TD

SAUVAGES
Marie-Madeleine Sauvages of Acadie, baptism 14 Oct. 1692
at Quebec. No marriage listed. Source – TD

SAUVAGES
Marie-Marguerite, a Micmac, baptized 21 July 1705 at Ste-
Anne, Quebec. No parents or marriage listed. Source – TD

SAUVAGES
Marie-Marguerite, appartenant a M. Duplessis-Morampont,
born 1737, baptized 17 Feb. 1755 at Quebec. No marriage
listed. Source – TD

SAUVAGES
Marie-Mectilde (Sauvages) of Becancour, died 6 Sept. 1741 at
Quebec. No marriage listed. Source – TD

SAUVAGES
Marie-Pelagie of St-Francois, baptized 14 Jan. 1771 at St-
Joseph, Beauce, Quebec. No parents listed. Source – TD

SAUVAGES

Marie-Renee Sauvages, a Panise, appartenant a M. Damours de Clianccur, born 1713, baptism 2 March 1720 at Quebec. Source – TD

SAUVAGES

Marie-Therese, a Micmac, baptized 11 June 1746 at Quebec. No marriage listed. Source – TD

SAUVAGES

Marie-Therese, a Montagaise Indian, appartenant a Charles Brousseau, born 1729, baptized 27 Dec. 1744 at Quebec. No marriage listed. Source – TD

SAUVAGES

Marie-Ursule Sauvages, a Micmac, born 1690, baptism 4 August 1692 at Quebec. No marriage listed. Source – TD

SAUVAGES

Marie-Ursule Sauvages, an Abenaquise, born 4 Sept. 1706, baptism 19 Sept. 1706 at Quebec. No marriage listed. Source – TD

SAUVAGES

Marie-Victoire, a Panise Indian, appartenant a M. Daine, born 1729, baptized 6 Jan. 1743 at Quebec. No marriage listed. Source – TD

SAUVAGES

Mathias, acien chief of the Huron at Detroit, (Michigan) born 1697, died 4 Aug. 1747 at Quebec. No marriage listed. Source – TD

SAUVAGES

Michel, an Abenaquis, baptized 3 Jan. 1748 at St-Joseph, Beauce, Quebec. No parents or marriage listed. Source – TD

SAUVAGES
Michel Sauvages, an Abenaquis, baptism 1702, death 13 Feb.
1710 at Quebec. Source – TD

SAUVAGES
Michel Sauvages, a Algonquin, baptism 10 Sept. 1727 at
Quebec. Source – TD

SAUVAGES
Michel, baptized 25 March 1710 at St-Pierre, Quebec.
Source – TD

SAUVAGES
Michel, an Abenaquis Indian, baptized 9 Aug. 1745 at
Quebec. No marriage listed. Source – TD

SAUVAGES
Michel, a Montagnais, born 1732, died 22 Feb. 1747 at
Quebec. Source – TD

SAUVAGES
Nicolas, a Montagnais, baptism 1709, death 28 Nov. 1714 at
Quebec. Source – TD

SAUVAGES
Nicolas Sauvages, baptism 24 Dec. 1700 at Quebec. No
marriage listed. Source – TD

SAUVAGES
Paul, baptized 30 Nov. 1730 at Lachine. No parents listed.
Source – TD

SAUVAGES
Paul-Charles, a Panis Indian, appartenant a M. Francois Chalet,
Director-General of the Campain des Indes, born 1730, baptized
28 April 1748 at Quebec. No marriage listed. Source – TD

SAUVAGES
Pierre, a Patacas, appartenant a M. Petrimoulx, born 1722, baptized 4 April 1733 at Quebec. Source – TD

SAUVAGES
Pierre, son of Pierre-Jacques and Marie-Joseph, abenaquis of St-Francois, baptized 22 Sept. 1771 at St-Joseph, Beauce, Quebec. No spouse of last name listed. Source – TD

SAUVAGES
Pierre, an Abenaquis, died 24 Oct. 1760 at St-Joseph, Beauce, Quebec. No parents listed. Source – TD

SAUVAGES
Pierre, a Montagnais, baptized 13 June 1734 at Kamouraska, Quebec. No parents listed. Source – TD

SAUVAGES
Pierre, appartenant a M. Philibert, born 1727, died 30 July 1738 at Quebec. Source – TD

SAUVAGES
Pierre, an Arkansas, baptized 29 June 1718 at Lachine. No parents listed. Source – TD

SAUVAGES
Pierre, died 18 Dec. 1745 at St-Joseph, Beauce, Quebec. No parents listed. Source – TD

SAUVAGES
Pierre, an Amalecite, died 28 May 1736 at Kamouraska, Quebec. No parents listed. Source – TD

SAUVAGES
Pierre, died 27 Sept. at Ste-Anne, Quebec. No parents listed. Source – TD

SAUVAGES
Pierre, appartenant a M. Vaudreuil, born 1717, died 3 May
1721 at Quebec. Source – TD

SAUVAGES
Pierre-Anbroise, an Abenaquis, baptized 1753, died 21 Feb.
1761 at St-Joseph, Beauce, Quebec. No parents listed.
Source – TD

SAUVAGES
Pierre-Andre Sauvages, a Caraibe, appartenant a M. Pierre
Jouanne, born 1712, baptism 23 Sept 1722 at Quebec.
Source – TD

SAUVAGES
Pierre, chief of the Micmac, par la cour, born 1678, died 8
June 1748 at Quebec. No marriage listed. Source – TD

SAUVAGES
Pierre Sauvages, an Abenaquis, baptism 3 July 1711 at
Quebec. No marriage listed. Source – TD

SAUVAGES
Pierre Sauvages, a Panis, appartenant, au gouverneur de
Vaudreuil, born 1716, baptism 22 Sept. 1719 at Quebec.
Source – TD

SAUVAGES
Pierre, an Amalecite, baptized 1756, died 10 June 1760 at St-
Joseph, Beauce, Quebec. No parents listed. Source – TD

SAUVAGES
Pierre, an Amalecite, baptized 1758, died 22 May 1760 at St-
Joseph, Beauce, Quebec. No parents listed. Source – TD

SAUVAGES
Pierre Sauvages, a Panis, bor 1711, baptism 16 Oct. 1717 at
Quebec. Source – TD

SAUVAGES
Pierre Sauvages, baptism 1693, died 21 Dec. 1702 at Quebec.
Source – TD

SAUVAGES
Pierre Sauvages, an Abenaquis, baptism 23 March 1710 at
Quebec. No marriage listed. Source – TD

SAUVAGES
Pierre-Bernard, a Micmac, baptized 27 Dec. 1731 at
Kamouraska, Quebec. No parents listed. Source – TD

SAUVAGES
Pierre-Jacques, baptized 11 June 1768 at St-Joseph, Beauce,
Quebec. No parents listed. Source – TD

SAUVAGES
Pierre-Jean, an Abenaquis, baptized 7 Aug. 1748 at Quebec.
Source – TD

SAUVAGES
Pierre-Jean Sauvages, an Abenaquis, baptism 30 June 1722 at
Quebec. Source – TD

SAUVAGES
Pierre-Louis Sauvages, a Cascaret-Panis, de la Louisianne,
baptism 25 Aug. 1718 at Quebec. (Pierre Haimard, ecolier,
pensionaire du seminaire at Quebec, fut son parrain).
Source – TD

SAUVAGES
Pierre-Marie, baptized 17 Nov. 1776 at St-Joseph, Beauce, Quebec. No parents listed. Source – TD

SAUVAGES
Pierre-Nicolas, baptized 10 Dec. 1758 at St-Joseph, Beauce, Quebec. No parents or marriage listed. Source – TD

SAUVAGES
Pierre-Noel, a Micmac, baptized 1737, died 1 Feb. 1738 at Kamouraska, Quebec. No parents listed. Source – TD

SAUVAGES
Pierre-Rene, baptized 14 Aug. 1757, aux Eboulements. No parents or marriage listed. Source – TD

SAUVAGES
Quatre, a sauvages, died 23 Feb. 1759 at Kamouraska, Quebec (L'acte dit: don't deux grands, un moyen et un petit.) No parents listed. Source – TD

SAUVAGES
Sebastien, an Abenaquis, baptized 1721, died 25 Feb. 1761 at St-Joseph, Beauce, Quebec. No parents or marriage listed. Source – TD

SAUVAGES
Six sauvages of Acadie, baptized 18 Sept. 1773 at St-Joseph, Beauce, Quebec. No parents listed. Another six enfants listed as baptized 1 Nov. 1773 at St-Joseph, Beauce. These could be number of children possibly orphaned? Plus another Deux (2) enfants baptized and died on 1 Nov. 1773 there too. And another Quatre enfants baptized 12 Dec. 1773, same place. Another Deux (2) enfants who baptized and died 30 Jan. 1774. Source – TD

SAUVAGES
Sauzanne, a Panise, appartenant a Jean Rochon, pere, born 1734, baptized 29 March 1748 at Lachenaye. No parents listed. Source – TD

SAUVAGES
Suzanne, an Abenaquise of the village of St-Francois, baptized 29 June 1763 at St-Joseph, Beauce, Quebec. No parents listed. Source – TD

SAUVAGES
Therese, appartenant of M. De la Richardiere, born 1735, baptized 22 July 1742 at Ste-Anne-de-la-Perade, Quebec. No marriage listed. Source – TD

SAUVAGES
Therese of Acadie, baptized 28 Oct. 1745 at St-Joseph, Beauce, Quebec. No parents or marriage listed. Source – TD

SAUVAGES
Therese-Francoise Sauvages, a Panise, born 1698, baptism 16 Feb. 1709 at Quebec. No marriage listed. Source – TD

SAUVAGES
Thomas, an Oneyouth, born 1719, died 3 Feb. 1749 at Quebec. Source – TD

SAUVAGES
Toussaint, an Algonquin, baptized 25 Sept. 1730 at St-Francois, I. J. No parents listed. Source – TD

SAUVAGES
Ursule, appartenant a Francois Devienne, born 1741, baptized 7 Aug. 1754 at Quebec. No marriage listed. Source – TD

SAUVAGES

Ursule-Cecile, died 16 Nov. 1748 at Quebec. Source – TD

SAUVAGES

Un Chef, of the Mission at Sault, died 19 Oct. 1702 at Quebec (en presence d'un grand nombre de temoins). Source – TD

SAUVAGES

Un Sauvage, an Abenaquis, born 1656, died 7 March 1766 at Ste-Anne-de-la-Pocatiere, Quebec. No marriage listed.
Source – TD

SAUVAGES

Un Sauvages of Miramichi (New Brunswick), died 30 July 1759 at Ste-Foye, Quebec. No parents or marriage listed.
Source – TD

SAUVAGES

Un, a Savage, appartenant a M. Foucault, born 1732, died 6 Jan. 1737 at Quebec. Source – TD

SAUVAGES

Un Sauvage, an Oneyout prisoner de guerre, died 10 March 1748 at Quebec. Source – TD

SAUVAGES

Un Sauvage, a Tsonnontouan, born before 25 Nov. 1731, Baptized 25 Nov. 1731 (dans) in prison and died 2 Dec. 1747 at Quebec. Source – TD

SAUVAGES

Un, sauvage et une sauvagesse, appartenant a M. Etienne Desroches, born 1739, died 16 Sept. 1744 at Quebec.
Source – TD

SAUVAGES
Un sauvages, venu du Lac Champlain, born 1745, died 24 August 1746 at Quebec. Source – TD

SAUVAGES
Un, sauvage, venu du Lac Champlain, born 1741, died 24 August 1746 at Quebec. Source – TD

SAUVAGES
Une, sauvagesse (Female), born 1706, died 1 Sept. 1746 at Quebec. No marriage listed. Source – TD

SAUVAGES
Un sauvage, born 1750, died 26 Aug. 1757 at Quebec. Source – TD

SAUVAGES
Un Garcon, born 1714, baptism 25 Oct. 1720 at Quebec. No marriage listed. Source – TD

SAUVAGES
Victor, Natches, born 1712, baptized 27 Aug. 1745 at Quebec. (Filleul de M. Varia de la Mare). No marriage listed. Source – TD

SAUVAGESSE
Une Sauvagesse (Female), appartenant a M. Lamotte, medecin, baptized 1735, died 30 March 1757 at Lachenaye. No parents listed. Source – TD

SEGUIN - SAUVAGE
Joseph Seguin, born 13 Sept. 1694, son of Francois Seguin Dit Laderoute and Jeanne Petit married 12 April 1723 to Francoise Sauvage of Detroit. Source – TD

SERREAU – MALECITE
Charles Serreau dit Saint-Aubin, son of Jean Serreau and Marguerite Boileau married 1690 to a Malecite girl. Children were: Joseph, b.c. 1708 St-Aubin; Jean-Baptiste, b.c. 1708 River Saint Jean (John), (New Brunswick). Source – DGDFA

SHEWARNETH – MEKESENAK
Charles Shewarneth, son of John-Baptiste Shewarneth (Abenaki) and Suzanne married Catherine Mekesanak, daughter of Joseph Mekesenak (Abenaki) and Marie (Sauvagesse) 24 Oct. 1781 at Becancour, Quebec. Source – MBQ

SHINING - ITAGISSE-CHRETIENNE
Jean-Baptiste Shining, husband of Francoise (Jumping) Itagisse-Chretienne. Source – TD

SIA8ABRK8E
Marie Sia8abrk8e, an Algonquine, died 7 Feb. 1698 age 90 at Montreal, Quebec. Source – TD

SIOU
Siou, age 40, embassador (rest in French - en ce pays, qui eut le bonheur d'eire baptise, et mouru; chez M. Le Scieur, interprete du dit Sauvage;) died 3 Feb. 1696 at Montreal, Quebec. Source – TD

SIOUSE
Agnes Siouse, appartenant a M. Normandin, baptized 1733, died 16 Dec. 1755 at Lachenaye. No parents listed. Source – TD

SIOUSE
Marie-Suzanne Siouse, appartenant a Jean-Baptiste Dumont, born 1731, baptized 4 May 1747 at Quebec. No marriage listed. Source – TD

SOIAGA
Soiaga Dit LeRat, Gaspard, chief of the Hurons at Michillimackinn died 3 Aug. 1701 at age 75 years at Montreal, Quebec. Source – TD

SOLOMON - AGIBCOCONA (Female)
Born 7 April 1799, Drummond Island, Michigan. Died 11 Feb. 1876, St. Joseph Island, Canada. She married, William Solomon. Their daughter was, Marie Jessie Louise Solomon who married Colbert/Albert/Cuthbert Amiot Sr. 3 Jan. 1837. He was born 21 March 1795 at Montreal, Quebec, Canada to Jean Baptiste Amiot, b. 1766, and Marie Archange Boucher who were married 1788. Jean B. was son of Jean Amoit and Marie LaVigne. Source – BKR

SOQUOQUIS, THERESE
Soquoquis. Was listed as 7 years old at St-Francois-du-Lac, Quebec with father, Mascoromeni (Soquoquis) and mother, Matecouat (Soquoquis) on 11 Feb. 1689. Source – JR

ST. CASTIN - PIDIANISKE
Baron de St. Castin, soldier and adventurer married Pidianiske, daughter of Madockawando (died c,\. 1698), last of the Wabanaki paramont-sakamos left in the Penobscot Bay area (Modern Castine, Maine). St. Castin was running a fur trading post. Source – LRM

ST. CASTIN
Vincent St. Castin, an Abenaquis, baptized 1741, died 6 June 1761 at St-Joseph, Beauce, Quebec. No parents or marriage listed. Source – TD

ST CERNY – PANISE

Pierre St. Cerny married Elizabeth Isabelle Carpentier Panise
(Indian) (Page 688). PRDH references:
http://www.leveillee.net/ancestry/actes/individu109847.htm
and http://www.leveillee.net/ancestry/famille5215.htm
and http://www.leveillee.net/ancestry/actes/famille15316.htm
Indicate that her name was Mary Élisabeth Isabelle
CARPENTIER. The "panise" is the name of a Native
American Tribe. Actually according to my research Pierre was
called Pierre Delpée dit St-Cerny.
Source – TD & LEV & PRDH

TAPENANIKOUE

Jean-Baptiste Tapenanikoue, an Algonquin, born 6 Sept. 1695
at Montreal, Quebec. Source – TD

TATOUEGOU

Charles Tatougou, born 27 March 1666 at Chateau-Richer,
Quebec. Source – TD

TAXOUS

Pierre (Taxous) Sauvage, an Abenaquis, born Feb. 1709 at
Acadie, baptism 23 Aug. 1709 at Quebec. No marriage listed.
Source – TD

TCHAATOREN (SAUVAGES) - GAENDI

Joseph Tchaatoren married Marie Gaendi. Children were:
Therese-Charlotte, b. 4 March 1678 at Quebec; Marie-Renee,
13 June 1679; Marie-Louise, b. 28 April 1680. Source – TD

TEGANNAC8AGHE

Iroquois du Sault Tegannac8aghe, born 1678, died 2 June
1703 at Montreal, Quebec. Source – TD

TEGOUI
Rene (Tegoui), an Abenaquis of Becancour, baptized 1700, died 15 Jan. 1745 at Lachenaye. No parents or wife listed. Source – TD

TEK8ARIMATH
Michel Tek8arimath died 23 Jan. 1685 at Chateau-Richer, Quebec. Source – TD

TEREMONGOUKE (SAUVAGES)
Louise-Charlotte (Teremongouke) Sauvages of Acadie, baptism 28 Nov. 1714 at Quebec. No marriage listed. Source – TD

THOMAS – MIUS
Jean-Baptiste Thomas was a Micmac Amerindienne chief from River Port Royal (Acadie) area who married around 1708 Marie Mius, daughter of Philippe Mius and Marie (an Amerindienne). Children were: Anne; Gabriel, b.c. 1727; Olive, b.c. 1732. One possible record says Jean was the son of Anougimtes at Cap Sable in 1708 at age 22 along with his wife Marie age 16. He possibly could have also been the Baptiste Thomas, chief of the Indians on river of Port Royal who was a witness to the marriage of Rene Nectabo and Catherine An8tgin on 24 Aug. 1726.
Source – DGDFA & DGDFA Eng Sup

TO STOP - PANIC
Pierre To Stop, husband of Marie Panic grass. Source – TD

TROTIER (DES RUISSEAUX) – ROY
Alexis Trotier (Des Ruisseaux), son of Antoine Trotier and Catherine Lefebvre. He was a Negociant, Colonel and Captain in the militia who married M. Louide Roy, daughter of Pierre Roy and Marguerite Ouabankikoue (Indian) 6 Jan. 1735 at Detroit (Michigan). Source – DNCF

TURGIS – AMERINDIENNE
Charles (de LaTour) Turgis de Saint-Etienne, b.c. 1593 married #1 an unnamed Amerindienne in 1625 and #2 Francoise Marie Jacquelin 1640 and #3 Jeanne Motin de Reux 1653. Children were: Jeanne, b.c. 1626 who married Martin d'Aprendestiguy de Martignon; Antoinette; A daughter.
Source – DGDFA

TURPIN - FAFARD
Jean Baptiste Turpin born 5 May 1710, Fort Detroit, New France (Michigan), son of Alexander Turpin and Charlotte Beauvais of Montreal, Quebec married Marguerite Fafard (Metis) daughter of late Jean Fafard, born 1657, died 21 Dec. 1756, Fort Detroit and Marguerite Conique (Couck), born 1664, daughter of Pierre Couck. Please refer to http://www.leveillee.net/ancestry/d294.htm#marguerite and scroll down to the daughter Marguerite Fafard. And PRDH http://www.leveillee.net/ancestry/famille10647.htm. The error here is Jean-Baptiste's mother. She is Marguerite COUC dit LAFLEUR, fourth child of Pierre COUC & MITE8AMEG8K8E. See reference #1 just above.
Source – DGA & LEV & PRDH

VALO – SAUVAGESSE
...... Valo married Marie Sauvagesse, baptized 1668, Micmac, died 19 Aug. 1738 at St-Anne-de-le-Pocatiere. Child was Rene, married 14 June 1745 to Marie-Anne Minaoure at St-Joachim. Source – TD

VALO – SAUVAGESSE
(Unnamed) Valo married Marie Sauvagesse (Indian) Micmac. Date and location not given on page 1323 of source.
Source – DNCF

VALO – MINAOURE
Rene Valo, a Micmac married 14 June 1745 at St-Joachim to Marie-Anne Minaoure, a Micmac; venve de ….Janot. Child was Jean, died 6 Nov. 1746. Source – TD

VALO (THIGAN) – MINAOURE
Rene Valo (Thigan), a Micmac married M. Anne Minaoure, a Micmac 14 June 1745 at St. Joachim. Source – DNCF

VALO – SAUVAGESSE
Thigan Valo married Marie Sauvagesse (Indian)(Page 688). Source – TD

VAUDRY – BOURDON (SAUVAGESSE)
Guillaume Vaudry, son of Antoine married 25 May 1809 at Cakokia to Rosalie Bourdon, Sauvagesse, daughter of Joseph. She must have died before 1829 because Guillaume remarried 18 May 1829 to Judith Touchet, daughter of Joseph. No children listed. Source – TD

VILLENEUVE – NEVEU (8KABE)
Daniel-Gabrial Villeneuve, son of Cas…., baptized 1690 married 1717 to Domitilde Neveu (8kabe). Children were: Therese, died 24 Sept. 1718 at Montreal, Quebec, Jean-Baptiste, baptized 1723, married 23 Nov. 1761 to Marie-Amable Caiouot. Source – TD

VINCENT – MADOKAWANDO & PIDIWAMMISKWA
Ensign Jean Vincent d'Abbadie de Saint Castin, son of Jean-Jacques Vincent and Isabeau de Bearn de Bonasse served in the Carrignan-Salieres Regiment that was sent by King Louis XIV in 1665. Jean decided to say in Canada after 1668. He served in Acadie and was recalled as a legendary person. He married #1 in 1670 to Mathilda Madakawando an Abenaki, a daughter of the chief. He died in 1707. 10 Children by #1: Claire, b.c. 1671 who married Paul Meunier; A daughter who

married Mr. Meneux dit Chateauneuf; A daughter who married Philippe Meunier; Anastasie who married Alexandre Le Borgne de Belisle; Bernard, b.c. 1688; Bernard-Anselme, b.c. 1689 married Charlotte D'Amours de Chauffours; Jean-Pierre, b.c. 1692; Ursuline, b.c. 1696 who married Louis D'Amours de Chauffours; Joseph who married unnamed person in 1728; Barenos who married unnamed person in 1725. Vincent was the baron of Saint Castin.

Jean Vincent married #2 Marie Pidiwammiskwa. His first wifes sister, Children were: Therese d'Abbadie de Saint-Castin who married 4 Dec. 1707 to Philippe Mius at Pentagouet (Acadie); and another daughter.

Source – DGDFA & TGR & LRAMD

VINCENT

Jean Vincent, son of Pierre and Marie Vincent of Acadie, baptized 23 Oct. 1773 at St-Joseph, Beauce, Quebec.

Source – TD

VISSE – IROQUOISE

Julien Visse married M. Angelique Iroquoise (Indian). Date and location not given on page 1346 of source. Source TD states: Julien Visse, marries Marie-Angelique, a Iroquoise. Had child, Cecile, married 7 Feb. 1743 to Pierre Dicaire at Lac-des-Deux-Montagnes. Source – DNCF & TD

VOISINE – MARTIN-LACROIX

Pierre Voisine, a "Sauvage Panis" (Probably Indian) married M. Anne Martin-Lacroix, daughter of Charles Martin-Lacroix and Catherine Dupuy 12 Nov. 1703 at Boucherville. A Pierre is listed again in marriage to M. Jeanne Peras-Lafontaine, daughter of Pierre Peras-Lafontaine and Denise Lemaistre 23 Dec. 1709 at Laprairie. Source – DNCF

WANNANNEMIM

Jeanne Wannannemim, born 1 May 1698 at Montreal of the nation of Loups. (Following in French) agee de 50 ans prise en Nov. 1695 par les sauvages du Sault, filleule de M. Hardouin et de Marthe Mills, veuve Grant. Source – TD

YOU – SAUVAGESSE

Pierre You, baptized 1658, died 28 Aug. 1718 at Montreal married first to Elisabeth Sauvagesse, a Miami. They had a child, Marie-Anne, baptized 1694, married 15 Aug. 1718 to Jean Richard. Pierre married second to Madeleine Juste. Children were: Louise, baptized 21 March 1706, died 7 Sept. 1728; Marie-Catherine, baptized 10 Sept. 1708. Source – TD

YOU – SAUVAGESSE

Pierre You, son of Pierre You and M. Renee Turrot of St. Sauveur at Le Rochelle, Aunis, France. He was an officer who married Elisabeth Sauvagesse (Indian) of Miami Tribe. No date or location given on page 1352 of source.
Source – DNCF

Useful Locations on the History of Huron and Other Tribes on the Net

Wendat Dialects and the Development of the Huron Allance, by John Steckley of Humber College.
http://www.wyandot.org/wendat.htm

Going Native: Breeds, Bloods, Renegades and the Metis, by Tom Bacig, 1992.
http://www.d.umn.edu/~tbacig/writing/Metis/brdmetis.html

Metis Cultural and Heritage Resource Centre, Inc. Great site for all kinds of Metis interests.
http://www.metisresourcecentre.mb.ca/

The Jesuit Relations and Allied Documents, 1610-1791, Compiled and Edited by Reuben Gold Thwaites and published by The Burrows Brothers Company, Cleveland, Ohio.
http://puffin.creighton.edu/jesuit/relations/

History & Genealogy, Early French, Abenaki & American Ancestors, Acadia and Penobscot, Maine, USA 1613-1721, by Danielle Duval Lemtre.
http://www.geocities.com/strivingmom/

Get into the heart of our Native North American Lives and Living. Camp at, Sites et Srjours Amerindiens DAO8EOLI TSONONTWAN, Native American Cultural Site, located at 310 Koska, Wendake Huron, Quebec, Canada G0A 4V0. Phone 418-848-3100, Email rgsioui@sympatico.ca Website: http://www.quebecweb.com/tsonontwan/introang.html

Huron Cultural Society (A Living Site), 575 rue Stanislas-Kosca, Village-des-Hurons (Wendake), Quebec, Canada G0A 4V0. Phone 418-842-4308. Owner/Founder Mario Gros-Louis. Website: www.huron-wendat.qc.ca

Metis Families, By Gail Morin. Website: http://www.televar.com/~gmorin/

Loyalty is Everything

Paul J. Bunnell, FACG, U.E.

For the past twenty-five years, Paul has devoted himself to genealogy and Loyalist studies. Self educated, he later took credited classes from Brigham Young University at Provo, Utah, greatly improving his skills and knowledge in this field. His accomplishments are wide; awarded the Accreditation and Fellowship at the American College of Genealogists of Illinois, and certified and registered lineage member of The United Empire Loyalist Association of Canada, and The Hereditary Order of Descendants of The Loyalist and Patriots of The American Revolution.

He has held past and present memberships in over sixty genealogical and writing organizations around the world, including life long memberships and chairman positions. He is also certified with the International Ghost Hunters Society in Paranormal Investigation, and also as Ghost Hunter. He is wlso a registered BYU blood donor on their genealogical DNA study.

His speaking engagements have been in New Jersey, New York, Massachusetts, New Hampshire, Maine, Connecticut and New Brunswick, including TV interviews on Cape Cod, Mass. and Saint John, New Brunswick stations. In 1989, His Majesty The Prince Philip of Wales (England) accepted his first book, *Thunder Over New England, Benjamin Bonnell, The Loyalist*, at Buckingham Palace. He was also presented with the well known "Loyalist Pin" from the past Mayor, Elsie Wayne of Saint John, New Brunswick, Canada (The Loyalist City). Paul has also produced several Internet articles on genealogy, including Black Loyalist, and Bonnell/Bunnell Loyalists. And let's not forget the "Loyalist Ghost of Benjamin Bonnell." Publications are many; *Thunder Over New England*; *The New Loyalist Index's 1, 2, 3*; *American Migrations & Documents Guide*; *The House of Robinson of Rhode Island & Baltimore, Maryland*; *Life of a Haunted House, The Barnstable House*; *Cemetery Inscriptions of The Town of Barnstable, Mass*; *Acadian & Cajun Cooking & Home remedies*; *Research Guide to Loyalist Ancestors*; *Tumbleweed, The Nellie Markham Letters*; and many other books in progress.

Paul enjoys traveling around lecturing or selling books at his vendor table at conventions. He also does Loyalist research for others out of his very large home library. Most of his publications can be ordered from Heritage Books, Inc., Westminster, Maryland, or all books from the author.

Paul's website is: www.bunnellgenealogybooks.Citymaker.com